D1497848

Overcoming Mobbing

Overcoming Mobbing

A Recovery Guide for Workplace Aggression and Bullying

MAUREEN DUFFY

LEN SPERRY

OXFORD
UNIVERSITY PRESS

OXFORD
UNIVERSITY PRESS

Oxford University Press is a department of the University of Oxford.
It furthers the University's objective of excellence in research, scholarship,
and education by publishing worldwide.

Oxford   New York
Auckland   Cape Town   Dar es Salaam   Hong Kong   Karachi
Kuala Lumpur   Madrid   Melbourne   Mexico City   Nairobi
New Delhi   Shanghai   Taipei   Toronto

With offices in
Argentina   Austria   Brazil   Chile   Czech Republic   France   Greece
Guatemala   Hungary   Italy   Japan   Poland   Portugal   Singapore
South Korea   Switzerland   Thailand   Turkey   Ukraine   Vietnam

Oxford is a registered trademark of Oxford University Press
in the UK and certain other countries.

Published in the United States of America by
Oxford University Press
198 Madison Avenue, New York, NY 10016

Library of Congress Cataloging-in-Publication Data
Duffy, Maureen P.
Overcoming mobbing : a recovery guide for workplace aggression and bullying / Maureen
Duffy, Len Sperry.—1 Edition.
  pages cm
Includes index.
ISBN 978–0–19–992955–9 (hardback : alk.
paper)   1. Bullying.   2. Harassment.   3. Bullying—Prevention.   I. Sperry,
Len.   II. Title.
BF637.B85.D856 2014
302.3'5—dc23
2013024077

9 8 7 6 5 4 3 2 1
Printed in the United States of America
on acid-free paper

To our life partners, Patrick and Patti
For everything

Contents

Foreword

Let me start with a confession. This is the book Ruth and I should have written years ago. We last revised our self-help book for targets of workplace bullying in 2009. Now comes this masterpiece by Maureen Duffy and Len Sperry, the essential guide for anyone interested in why and how workplace abuse happens and how to get past it in their lives.

Readers, you are in good hands. The information between the covers is absolutely spot-on. You can place your trust in these two authors. And, for a bonus, organizations get advice, too. The authors' trustworthiness derives from 30 years of immersion as clinicians and consultants dealing with mental health, organizational issues, and workplace health and aggression and caring for vulnerable former employees who experienced the mistreatment so thoroughly described in these pages.

Practical is the adjective that best describes this book. Though it is rich in citations and relies on science, applicability to real lives, real families, and real organizations jumps off the pages. It tackles an admittedly complex subject with an accessible writing style that showcases illustrations, summary lists, and tables. Points are driven home artfully with compassion for victims present throughout.

What makes this book a remarkable work is the seamless marriage between the disciplines of clinical psychology, social psychology, and organizational consulting. Each domain informs readers with different needs. Anecdotal tales of mobbing and abuse enliven the book. Victim-targets will see themselves portrayed in illustrative case studies such as those of Linda, who believed in fairness; the micromanaged Jim; Dwayne, the sacked coach; postal worker Tom McIlvaine; physician Laurel; and the prototypical mobbed victim from Chapter 4. The cases, written with obvious authenticity, will validate targets.

Duffy and Sperry are brave collaborators. They challenge contemporary American media distortions, and thus publicly held notions, that workplace abuse is the product of a few evil, malevolent abusers. They characterize this specialized type of aggression as a form of nonphysical violence suffered in silence by victims because of its routine nature, accepted as the American way of doing work. They pull the curtain back to reveal mobbing as the complex interaction of factors and forces in the workplace that it truly is. There are important lessons for both mobbed individuals and organizational representatives who genuinely strive to identify root causes of destructive interpersonal conduct.

For individuals, naming what happened to them and correctly placing the source of their misery outside themselves is the first step toward recovery. Chapter 1 helps victims accomplish that task. Without externalizing the mobbing, targets are doomed to ruminate and wonder ceaselessly about what they did to deserve their fate. In our work, we find it helpful to teach targets about the fundamental attribution error as the root of victim denigration. The authors describe that phenomenon in the clearest language I've ever read.

Duffy and Sperry creatively describe how being "different" is often the triggering event in mobbing, and how others perceive targets as different can be surprising. Chapter 4 provides the lucid reality of mobbing as seen through the lens of the victim. Clearly the authors' clinical acumen informs the details. Our work with thousands of targets matches perfectly the vivid illustration of how competent adults are reduced to humiliated, self-doubting shells of their former selves. The authors kindly caution victims to read the accounts of what happens and how health is adversely affected carefully in case personal trauma is retriggered.

This is the only major book to provide family members a guide to understanding what happened to their mobbed spouse or parent. In addition, suggestions for ways to communicate fears and questions are provided. The advice in Chapter 6 makes an invaluable contribution to the literature.

In cases of full-blown mobbing, the lone individual is up against several people in the organization at different levels, all focused on driving him or her from the workplace. The "ganging up" escalates when higher-level management gets involved. The orchestrated effort by many against one eventually deprives the unsuspecting and innocent victim-target of health and well-being, income, status, health insurance (a uniquely American consequence), the ability to financially and emotionally support a family, and sometimes a career. The devastation is predicted in sobering Chapters 5 and 6.

The blunt and truthful authors then describe how organizations create "shadow files" and do whatever it takes to allow administrators to hide behind the myth that the organization is a "good and fair place to work." Hypocritically, those employers discard good employees as though they are dispensable resources using the tactics of mobbing fueled by the hurtful power of social exclusion and ostracism.

The authors do not leave the reader submerged in the dark side of the world of work. Ultimately, the book is about hope and inspiration. The seventh chapter signals the shift toward a discussion of recovery from mobbing. The valuable advice flows steadily and includes gems such as "don't make fighting the organization that mobbed you your next career." Their wisdom extends to selecting psychotherapists who practice "trauma-informed mental health care" by taking into account the organizational, cultural, and power dynamics that instigated the mobbing experience rather than focusing on the victim's vulnerability.

Personal recovery from mobbing is best exemplified by reengagement in life, again finding meaning and purpose. The authors wisely advise former victims to practice patience because recovery is a long process. The ten principles given in Chapter 7 combined with the recovery tools listed in Chapter 8 allow victims to work at their own pace to reclaim their lives after mobbing.

Trusting others again is a hurdle that has to be overcome to live fully, and social support is the antidote to stress. The authors explain how to build one's "mobbing recovery support team." Reversing isolation is critical, and instructions are given as to how to accomplish it. All of the other tools are certain to aid recovery, especially sharing judiciously with selected others one's previously unilateral dialogue about the experienced trauma.

The authors defiantly critique the "bad apple," personality-dominated explanation for mobbing. They give the reader an introduction to work environments and their working parts. Personalities of perpetrators comprise only a small part.

Hooray for Duffy and Sperry's clarity in pronouncing that banishing bullies does not end the systemic problem. As the authors write, "It takes an organization" to create it, and that's what it takes to stop it.

The discussion about transforming workplaces from mobbing-prone to mobbing-resistant begins in Chapter 9. Examples of both types are showcased—Florida A&M University and Catholic Health Services, respectively. The authors introduce a concept foreign to American corporations, organizational health, and provide an instrument to assess it. Advice for employers ends with four takeaway points worth their weight in gold.

Let's hope internal champions of anti-abuse initiatives grab a copy of this book for tips and validation. They, and not the majority in business, are doing the right thing. As the authors write, developing an intolerance of mobbing "does involve deliberate mindfulness of the impact of workplace behavior on other people and their families." The authors call on coworkers to act ethically. I agree that witnesses possess untapped power but nevertheless fail to intervene. If only they would! Finally, the authors suggest that responsible organizations that mobbed their workers should make the injured whole and ensure restorative justice. From the pen of Duffy and Sperry to American business leaders everywhere...

Gary Namie, PhD
Workplace Bullying Institute

Preface

In *Overcoming Mobbing: A Recovery Guide for Workplace Aggression and Bullying* you will be introduced to a concept that you may be seeing for the first time—that of *mobbing*, in particular, workplace mobbing. If you have never seen or heard of the concept before you are probably reading this book because you are interested in the topic of workplace abuse. Mobbing refers to a type of workplace abuse that, unfortunately, is fairly common. In fact, much of what is referred to as workplace bullying is more accurately described, as we will explain in these pages, as workplace mobbing. Mobbing is a complex phenomenon that happens in workplaces and in other settings and that involves individuals, groups, and the larger organization mutually influencing the behavior of one another. Most workplace abuse involves the interaction of individuals, groups, and organizations and is not just the product of a single bully or small group of bullies directing their aggression toward a hapless victim.

Unfortunately, when it is mentioned in the media, mobbing and bullying are often misrepresented and misportrayed. You may recall a reporter or columnist beginning a story with: "Remember that big kid who shook you down for your lunch money when you were in third grade? Well, guess what, he's now the bully in the Brooks Brothers' suit in the office down the hall from yours." Such "once a bully, always a bully" thinking is not supported by the research. That's because mobbing has many causes beyond the personality characteristics of an individual. Those causes include the way in which individuals, groups, and organizations influence each other in particular situations. By the time you finish reading *Overcoming Mobbing*, your image of bullying and what a bully is will be different from the stereotype of a powerful boss screaming at a cowering and browbeaten worker.

Understanding workplace mobbing requires accepting its complexity and the roles that individuals, groups of workers, management and administration, and the organization itself, with its unique history and culture, all play in its development. If workplace abuse could be explained by pointing to a "bad apple" or "rotten egg," an individual offender or small group of offenders, then most bullies would have been cleared out of organizations by now and workplace abuse would be a thing of the past. But that clearly is not the case. Understanding workplace abuse and, in particular, workplace mobbing, requires looking not only at how individuals can behave abusively but also at how individuals gang up in groups at work, and how organizational leadership and authority become involved in behaviors that harm targeted workers. This book, therefore, is not about blaming. It's about understanding and healing—understanding what workplace mobbing is and how it happens and what to do to recover if you or a loved one has been impacted by it.

Where Our Explanations Go Wrong

For a number of reasons, the first impulse of the general public, most managers, many psychotherapists, and almost all the media is to attribute workplace mobbing to the negative personality characteristics of the individual offender or offenders. In terms of explanatory power, this "bad apple" explanation is quite limiting; however, it is consistent with the emphasis on individualism reflected in ideas like the "American Dream." Our societal sense of rugged individualism has us overemphasizing the role of the individual in both success and failure and underemphasizing the broader social context in which both success and failure happen. The "bad apple" view can help us to feel better after we hear about disturbing events in which people have gotten hurt either psychologically or physically. All we have to do is figure out who is to blame and separate that person in some way. If we believe that an individual alone is responsible for something bad and we know who that individual is, then the problem is more or less solved.

This "bad apple" view reflects a mental bias that most Westerners hold. It is a bias toward being comfortable with explanations that emphasize individual psychological factors over explanations that also include more complex situational and contextual factors. Social psychologists refer to this bias or "bad apple" viewpoint as the *fundamental attribution error*.[1,2] In a nutshell, the fundamental attribution error is the tendency for individuals to overemphasize personality-based explanations in others while underemphasizing the importance of situational and organizational influences. According to this bias, individuals assume that the actions of others are indicative of the type of people they are rather than of the social and organizational forces that influence them. Not surprisingly, this assumption can result in our making erroneous explanations about behavior. Ironically, this bias of overemphasizing personality-based explanations is less likely to occur when individuals evaluate their own behavior. When people look at their own behavior they are more likely to consider situational and contextual elements that have influenced them than when they are evaluating someone else's behavior.

Conversely, other explanations take into account the complexity of human behavior and include the power of groups, organizations, and communities in influencing behavior. We utilize these explanations, which acknowledge that both groups and organizations influence the behavior of individuals within them, in understanding and analyzing workplace mobbing. Workplace mobbing is a complex phenomenon that is inadequately explained by only looking at individual behavior. In fact, it takes looking at the interaction of three different levels of explanation to adequately understand workplace mobbing. Ultimately, three sets of explanations are required to provide a reasonably coherent and compelling account of workplace mobbing:

    (1) the individual dynamics, or "bad apple" view,
    (2) the work group dynamics, or the "some bad apples" view, and
    (3) the organizational dynamics, or the "bad barrel" view.

A basic premise of this book is that three sets of dynamics influence an individual's behavior in a workplace setting: personality or individual dynamics, situational or group dynamics, and systemic or organizational dynamics. Think of dynamics as influencing or motivating characteristics. To fully comprehend and explain behavior in an organizational or community setting, all three sets of dynamics must be considered, not just one or two. A related premise is that individual, group, and organizational dynamics can either foster or reduce the likelihood of mobbing in the workplace.

Typically, particularly with regard to cases of abusive and even violent workplace behavior, the media provide us with biased "either-or" explanations that are not helpful in understanding workplace mobbing, in recovering from it, or in effectively preventing it. They neither provide us with a name (mobbing) for this phenomenon, nor do they help us understand that mobbing is an ongoing process and not simply a culminating event, for instance the termination of a previously valued employee on a particular day or, in the worst cases, a suicide or shooting spree on a particular day.

To the extent that we uncritically accept limiting explanations and information voids we are likely to reconfirm our biases and ideologies. The result of uncritical acceptance of incomplete information is that we can become accustomed to thinking that we understand complex issues when we really do not. Unfortunately, this means that any decisions we might make about policies or the actions we take based on incomplete or inaccurate information are likely to be shortsighted, ineffective, or possibly even harmful. What we need at this point is a comprehensive perspective about workplace mobbing and related abusiveness.

Plan of the Book

In *Overcoming Mobbing* you will find a different point of view from much of what you may have been led to believe about workplace abuse. It provides a critical and thorough perspective on workplace mobbing and related forms of abusiveness. You will find information in the pages that follow that is based on clinical practice, current theory, research, and technical information gathered in the United States and from around the world. You will also find several case illustrations combined with helpful analyses, as well as practical guidelines and tips for recognizing, dealing with, recovering from, and preventing mobbing.

In writing *Overcoming Mobbing* we had a number of goals. One was to provide a comprehensive description of workplace mobbing in as clear a way as possible so that readers will be able to recognize it when they see it. Another goal was to provide an understanding of the effects of workplace mobbing on victims, their families, bystanders, and on the organizations within which it occurs. A very important goal for us and one for which there didn't seem to be much of a path to follow was identifying practical strategies for both individuals and organizations so that they can recover from mobbing.

The strategies that we developed for recovery from workplace mobbing are grounded in our clinical and consulting experience of thirty years and shaped by the body of knowledge referred to as *trauma-informed care and practice*.[3] Our recovery strategies are also shaped by work in social psychology in the area of *social exclusion*.[4,5] This work has important relevance for research and practice in workplace mobbing since exclusion is both a means and the endgame of mobbing. Through our focus on individual, family, and organizational recovery we have tried to identify potential intervention points where healing and positive change are both possible and realistic.

From the many people who have read our previous book or articles about mobbing and communicated with us, we know that it has been enormously helpful for them to find information about the topic and to feel that their own painful experiences of workplace mobbing have been validated. That being said, workplace mobbing by its nature is a difficult topic. Therefore, if reading this book or using some of our mobbing recovery strategies and tools increases distress in any way we recommend putting the book aside and seeking professional help and social support and picking the book up again when it is comfortable to do so.

While in *Overcoming Mobbing* we confront and name the pain and losses involved in workplace mobbing, this book is ultimately about recovery, healing, and realistic hope for a better future for individuals, families, and organizations affected by it. Our primary focus is on workplace mobbing, but the recovery principles and strategies that we describe are also relevant for workplace bullying and other forms of workplace aggression and abuse. The aggression to which we refer in this book is aggression that is primarily psychological and not physical in nature.

The case illustrations that you will read in this book are derived from the perspectives of mobbing "insiders." Mobbing insiders include victims, perpetrators, witnesses or bystanders, and those holding organizational authority when a mobbing occurred. Heinz Leymann, who did the pioneering research on workplace mobbing, cautioned his readers that if they think they recognize a case, they should assume that they are wrong. Leymann advised that many cases of workplace mobbing sound similar because the employer or organization is determined to get rid of a particular person and there are only so many ways to do that.[6] Leymann was astute in recognizing that the process of ostracizing and eliminating a targeted worker from the workplace through workplace mobbing can only take on a limited number of forms, and therefore many cases resemble each other. Our work and analysis confirm Leymann's view, and we underscore his reminder.

Both the terms *victim* and *target* are used to describe the subject of workplace mobbing or other workplace abuse. Both terms make sense to us, and either is appropriate as a descriptor of the subject of workplace mobbing. We use *victim* more frequently than *target* as a way of highlighting that workplace mobbing results in victimization, which, in turn, results in injury. We do not view victims of injury as feeling sorry for themselves or as having chosen a career as a victim as do some in popular culture. Our use of the term *victim* is to remind us all that victimization from workplace mobbing can result in injury no less than from accidents or violence, albeit that the injury is usually of a psychological nature.

While mobbing and bullying are forms of abusiveness and share some similarities, many differences exist between them, and so the importance of distinguishing these two phenomena is the focus of the first chapter. For now we can say that the difference between the two is that mobbing always involves organizational dynamics, whereas bullying does not. We would also add that distinguishing mobbing from bullying is critical for the process of successfully recovering as well as in preventing both.

While one or two of the stories and examples in this book are dramatic, headline-grabbing illustrations of mobbing, most are so commonplace that they may only be reported a time or two in your local news, if at all. These common, everyday examples with no external drama or lawsuits are how mobbing is experienced by most Americans. Because workplace mobbing is commonplace, we want you to be able to recognize and name this form of mental violence and have a variety of resources for dealing with it, recovering from it, and even preventing it from happening to you.

Acknowledgments

We acknowledge and thank the many people from around the world who have taken the time to share their stories with us of having been mobbed. We continue to deepen our understanding of the process of workplace mobbing, and we have learned much from the stories of their experiences. We hope that through this book we have helped to advance the understanding of what workplace mobbing is, how it affects targets and families, and what kind of interventions are both helpful and unhelpful. It is very important to us that health care providers do not unwittingly add insult to injury through lack of understanding of what workplace mobbing is and the trauma that often follows in its wake.

The foundation for understanding workplace mobbing was laid by the late Heinz Leymann and his colleagues in Sweden. His rich legacy of organizational and clinical research continues to inspire us and to help us in our efforts to more thoroughly understand and analyze workplace mobbing. Our contributions to the understanding of workplace mobbing have been greatly enhanced by the generative research and insight of Kenneth Westhues, University of Waterloo in Canada, and by his generosity and kindness of spirit. We offer our sincerest thanks and appreciation to him.

No one stands out more in advocating for bully-free and psychologically safe workplaces than do Ruth and Gary Namie and their colleagues at the Workplace Bullying Institute in Bellingham, Washington. We offer our sincerest thanks to them for both the work that they do and for the support that they have offered to us even as we may differ about the use of some terminology. We would also like to acknowledge David Yamada, professor of law and director of the New Workplace Institute at Suffolk University Law School in Boston, for his commitment and sensitivity to issues of justice in the workplace and for his pioneering work in authoring the Healthy Workplace Bill that has been introduced in a number of state legislatures. We also extend our appreciation to the anonymous reviewers of our book for their careful reviews and most helpful comments. We valued their insights and their important roles in helping us to improve our book.

I (MD) also express my appreciation and thanks to my husband, Patrick, for his unflagging support of my work and for his endless patience and good humor about my rather fixed location in front of my desk and window. To my sister, Eileen Alexander, I also offer thanks and appreciation for her wholehearted support and encouragement. To Len Sperry, my esteemed colleague and collaborator in our joint projects on workplace mobbing, I offer my thanks and appreciation for his careful analysis and insights, for his willingness to engage in spirited debate, and for our long and winding conversations that invariably take us into the most fascinating of conversational spaces. Finally, I thank Alaka McConnell (Alaka Pande), of the Workplace Mobbing and Bullying International Nurses Network and Support Group, for the helpful conversations that we have had and for her thoughtful ideas about the recovery process.

I (LS) again acknowledge my wife, Patricia, for your support of my research and writing efforts. Over all these years, your constant love and forbearance with projects like this means the world to me. To Maureen Duffy, my coauthor on this our second book, I want you to know how much I really enjoy collaborating with you. It is also fitting to acknowledge Steve Vensel, Ph.D., whom I supervised on his pioneering dissertation research on mobbing.

To our editor at Oxford University Press, Sarah Harrington, and our assistant editor, Andrea Zekus, we offer our gratitude for their support of our work, meticulous attention to detail, and belief in the importance of getting the word out about workplace mobbing and its destructive effects. Also at Oxford, we thank our production editor, Emily Perry, for handling all of the details required to transform these words and sentences into the beautiful book that it is.

Overcoming Mobbing

Mobbing Is Not Bullying

ORKPLACE MOBBING IS A DESTRUCTIVE SOCIAL process in which individuals, groups, or organizations target a person for ridicule, humiliation, and removal from the workplace. It is unlike anything most have ever experienced. Its victims, their family members, friends, and coworkers are frequently unable to make sense of the experience or to mobilize resources for recovery. It leaves the victim reeling, not knowing what has happened, why it happened, and, most important, what will happen in the future. Being mobbed can take away a victim's sense of safety and security in the world, sense of identity and belonging, and the belief that the world is a fair and just place. It frequently leads to deteriorating physical and mental health. Suicides and violence, including homicides, have occurred following mobbing. Inevitably, mobbing leaves a trail of devastation for victims, their family members, and the workplace organizations and institutions in which it occurs.

Mobbing is not about the occasional negative or even abusive experience at work. Most adult workers are sophisticated enough to understand that occasional intense and difficult interactions with coworkers and supervisors can and do happen, and they are mature enough to tolerate and cope fairly well with them. Mobbing is different. It is the experience of ongoing negative acts, both overt and covert, over time, which erodes workers' confidence in themselves and in their workplaces. No amount of sophistication or maturity can make sense of it.

The terms *workplace mobbing* and *workplace bullying* are often used interchangeably to refer to aggressive and abusive behavior at work. Reasonable people have debated and disagreed about which is the most accurate term to use. Some suggest that it doesn't matter whether workplace abuse is called *workplace mobbing* or *workplace bullying* because, in the end, abuse is abuse. We think it does matter—not because we want to be persnickety or difficult about the subject—but because we think that workplace mobbing and workplace bullying are two different kinds of abuse that can occur at work and that they involve the operation of different factors and dynamics. To look at the differences between workplace bullying and workplace mobbing, consider the following two workplace abuse situations.

Workplace Abuse Scenario One: Bullying

Jim was recently promoted to the public relations department in his tech company where he worked with a small group on preparation of written and graphic materials for distribution within the industry and to the public. His job description also included product research analysis. His new boss, Diane, had a reputation for being a stickler for detail. Jim was not concerned because he had a strong record of accomplishment in the company already and had earned a reputation for being able to work well under pressure and meet deadlines, even the tightest ones. Right off the bat, Diane gave Jim some fairly high-level projects involving the development of presentation materials and a product analysis booklet. Jim felt good about the confidence Diane had placed in him by assigning such important projects to him right away. He responded by getting to work on the projects immediately in his customary way.

The nitpicking and constant criticism started soon after. Diane wanted a progress report and work summary on the projects every afternoon. She complained to Jim about the approach he was taking with the product analysis; she complained about the graphics he chose to represent the key ideas; she complained about his writing style and didn't think he was producing enough volume on a daily basis. Diane set an arbitrary daily word count for Jim without consulting him and without taking into consideration which section of the project he was working on—some sections were much more complicated than others and would take longer to analyze and write up.

When Jim protested that the schedule for the projects didn't make sense, Diane cut him off and verbally warned him that the daily goals she had set were minimums and were not up for discussion. She also told him that she wanted all new graphics and that she wanted his writing style to be more formal. Although he didn't like it, Jim did his best to comply and brought his work product every afternoon to the progress meeting Diane had set up. Diane continued to criticize his layout, his graphics, his data charts, his writing style, his color and font choices, and his overall approach to the product analysis he was doing. Every day was a new complaint and a new criticism of his work. Jim was finding Diane unreasonable and impossible to work with, and his confidence in his own abilities was deteriorating.

Workplace Abuse Scenario Two: Mobbing

The chief operating officer (COO) of the company had a well-publicized open-door policy. The COO encouraged senior managers, middle managers, and even staff to stop by if they needed anything or if they had a problem that he could help them with. The COO liked to develop the illusion of an open-door policy even though what he was most open to was gossip about other members of the organization and the more salacious and malicious the better. He kept files of bits and pieces of information about organizational members that he thought might come in handy in the future should the need arise to use the information against someone.

If naïve staff members or middle managers had the temerity to stop by his office because of an actual concern that was impacting their work, the COO would invariably chastise them for not following the chain of command. The COO's open-door policy confused reporting relationships within the company, and although they would never admit it, company insiders knew all too well that the open door was frequently used for the dissemination of personal and professional gossip about others.

The COO's so-called open-door policy made it very easy to silence points of view that were not endorsed by the company and to target someone as a troublemaker. The COO was a gossipmonger disguised as a benevolent leader who made a point of collecting all kinds of information about organizational members, especially information about their "attitudes" and whether they were going along with organizational authority.

So when Linda's line manager went to the COO to complain about what he described as Linda's vocal and incessant challenging of company policy about how goal setting was used in performance reviews, the COO welcomed him with open arms. Linda's manager told the COO that Linda was stirring up other staff members in the department and that his verbal skills were not a match for hers, giving Linda the upper hand in staff meetings. He let the COO know in an indirect way, so that he could never be quoted, that he would prefer it if Linda were eased out of his department and preferably out of the company altogether.

For months, Linda had been complaining that goal setting in employee performance reviews and evaluations was being misused to document poor performance and highlight failure rather than to motivate and improve performance as originally intended. This was a nagging concern for Linda because she had been on the performance review and evaluation committee and knew that the customer service goals had been designed as aspirational targets rather than as actual performance benchmarks. Linda felt that she was letting down her coworkers by not pointing out that supervisors were misusing the goal-setting components of performance reviews to the detriment of all the employees.

The COO told the manager to start putting together a paper trail about Linda's inappropriate behavior and to interview other employees, both past and present, about what they thought of Linda, her job performance, and her customer service skills. Because Linda's job performance was in the above-average range based on standard evaluation metrics, the COO and her manager knew—although they never said it—that it was going to require a little more care to ease her out. (They had targeted personnel for job elimination before and were fairly skilled at it.)

Linda's manager decided to start gathering information about her from among the secretarial pool. He knew that one of the secretaries had it in for her and that it would be a perfect place to start the process of undermining her reputation. Even though Linda's manager would dutifully tell the secretary that his conversation with her was absolutely confidential, he knew that it would only be a matter of minutes after he left before this secretary, who trafficked in gossip, would gleefully start spreading the word that Linda was under investigation. Ironically, Linda's manager and the COO did not like or respect each other, but they had worked together to eliminate key staff members from the organization before, and in Linda's case, they were intent on doing it again.

Distinguishing Mobbing from Bullying

In Scenario One, the two key figures were Jim and his boss, Diane. The bullying relationship involved Diane, whom we can think of as the perpetrator, and Jim, whom we can think of as the victim. Diane engaged in supervisory behavior that was consistently hostile and critical and that failed to acknowledge Jim's job skills and strengths. Additionally, Diane's supervisory behavior was arbitrary and controlling. Jim's previous job performance was above average to excellent and provided no reasonable basis for the kind of close scrutiny to which he was subjected. He was not on a remediation plan requiring increased reporting in and supervision.

The arbitrariness of Diane's dislike of Jim's writing style and his choices for graphics and data displays together with her demand for an inflexible work volume that did not take into account the level of difficulty of a particular project could suggest issues of power and control on Diane's part. Diane's interactions with Jim also raise the possibility of a personality conflict with him, the possibility that she felt threatened by Jim's repertoire of skills, and, at the very least, show an overall deficit on Diane's part in project and personnel management skills. Diane's bullying behavior made work increasingly unpleasant for Jim and also affected his sense of confidence in his own abilities.

Diane's bullying behavior and poor supervisory skills were clear to Jim and became clear to Diane's manager when Jim eventually went over Diane's head to complain about his work situation and the hostile work climate in which he had unexpectedly found himself. While Diane's manager valued her and her contributions to the company, she also recognized that Jim had a legitimate set of concerns and that Diane could benefit from management coaching. Jim was relocated to a different department with no reduction in status or pay.

There was no effort to drive Jim from the organization or humiliate him through demotion or unfavorable disciplinary action, and his reputation as a high performer remained intact. There was also no ganging up on Jim by other coworkers or other managers and administrators. In Jim's case, the bullying situation was limited to an individual bully-boss who admittedly made Jim's life miserable while she remained his boss but whose impact on him was contained once he relocated to another department in the company at full status and pay. To prevent recurrence, Diane's bullying behavior needed to be addressed by the organization's management.

In Scenario Two, the abusive actions targeted against Linda were much more covert than those targeted against Jim in Scenario One. From shortly after the triggering conflict with her manager, the series of targeted, abusive actions toward Linda was sanctioned at the upper levels of the organization and were carried out by the COO, by Linda's line manager, by a secretary several rungs lower on the organizational chart, and, over time, grew to include her coworkers at the same organizational level. Linda's coworkers had begun to distance themselves from her after it became common knowledge that she had been labeled as a troublemaker and that she was under investigation.

The initial abusive acts included the deliberate gathering together of any unflattering information that the COO already had in his files about Linda and the tacit agreement between the COO and her line manager to do whatever was necessary to create a negative paper trail. These initial abusive acts were followed by the proactive gathering of more negative information about Linda through the manager's trumped-up investigation of what coworkers and subordinates thought about her, her job performance, and her customer service skills, and the leading questions that he used to question her coworkers about her. The purpose of the trumped-up investigation was deliberately vague and focused on Linda's personality and character more than on her job performance. Linda's outspokenness had gotten under her manager's skin, and this time he was determined to do something about it other than just complain that she was not a good "fit" for the department and for the company.

Consistent with the abusive behavior directed toward her, Linda was not notified that she was under investigation, trumped-up as the investigation was, and only learned through the company grapevine that her manager was interviewing others about her. Linda's manager used existing formal procedures for conducting disciplinary investigations, although he even corrupted those by failing to formally notify Linda of the fact that she was under disciplinary investigation and the reasons for the investigation. Informal organizational channels were used to spread gossip, innuendo, and character attacks and followed the track of naturally occurring groups, subgroups, coalitions, and alliances within the organization.

The initial phase of the workplace mobbing of Linda involved the undermining of her personal and professional reputation and the sowing of doubt about her credibility and stature within the organization. This phase took some time to thoroughly complete. After its completion, Linda left the organization in shame and disbelief, feeling betrayed by the company she had conscientiously worked for and by the coworkers with whom she had believed she had respectful working relationships. For her line manager, the COO, the secretary who defamed her, and her coworkers who abandoned her, it was mission accomplished. After Linda left the organization, some of the key actors in her mobbing self-righteously commented that she would be better off in a different organization and that she had contributed a lot to the company.

Workplace Mobbing: It Takes an Organization

The abusive behavior directed at Linda had little to nothing to do with her job performance and everything to do with her presentation of self and with her identity. Linda demonstrated the qualities of straightforwardness, bluntness, and independence that her Eastern European parents had prized and nurtured in her. She was not a "go with the flow" type of person and took things seriously, especially her work. She had always been kept at arm's length by her supervisors because she was known to speak her mind. Linda knew that her independent streak was not regarded as an asset in her organization, but she didn't know just how problematic it would turn out to be. Ultimately it would cost her both her job and her health. A toxic culture of gossip and defamation and an in-group/out-group mentality had persisted in the organization for years and had provided fertile ground for targeted attacks on individual employees both currently and in the past.

An individual bully-boss with personal issues around power and control did not target Linda. That would have been bad enough. She became victim to an organization whose leadership, structure, and culture allowed the concerns of a line manager to morph into an all-out campaign to get rid of her. In a nonabusive organization, the concerns of Linda's manager would have been handled very differently, starting from a standpoint of greater tolerance for diversity of opinion and expression of that opinion. After all, what triggered Linda's mobbing was her line manager's discomfort at her insistence that decisions about performance evaluation procedures that had already been made be followed. In reality, the problems were Linda's line manager's and not hers. But his organizational influence and power, which eventually got her labeled as a troublemaker, started the ball rolling that resulted in her being forced out of the organization after being subjected to ongoing abuse. For Linda to have been mobbed it took the organization.

Mobbing is not bullying. It is often far worse than bullying. Mobbing takes place within organizational or institutional settings and always includes organizational involvement. Key organizational members become involved in mobbing through overt or covert actions against a target or through failure to act to protect organizational members from abuse. Bullying is the subjecting of a targeted individual to hostile and abusive acts by one or more individuals without the presence of organizational involvement. The key distinction between bullying and mobbing is the absence of organizational involvement in bullying and the presence of organizational involvement in mobbing.

The presence of organizational involvement in mobbing compounds the injury to victims. It is not only the direct perpetrators who have inflicted harm and abuse on the target but also the organization itself through either its direct actions or its failure to act to stop the abuse and protect the target. In workplaces, individuals can bully and groups can bully. But once the weight and power of the organization becomes involved, it's no longer workplace bullying, it's mobbing.

Table 1.1 uses the workplace abuse scenarios previously described to compare and contrast workplace bullying and workplace mobbing across a range of factors. The differences between workplace bullying and workplace mobbing drawn from the analysis of the scenarios of Jim and Linda that are reflected in Table 1.1 are consistent with the distinctions between bullying and mobbing identified by other researchers in the field.[1,2]

There is no doubt that the incidents of both workplace bullying and workplace mobbing described above resulted in psychological harm to their respective victims and that both the bullying scenario and the mobbing scenario are instances of workplace abuse. It's also clear that misuse and abuse of power were present in both scenarios. But there are also important differences between the two scenarios that are reflective of the differences between workplace bullying and workplace mobbing.

Power and Workplace Mobbings

Let's start with the issue of power. Viewpoints about workplace bullying often assume a static power imbalance between the perpetrator and the victim where the perpetrator has more power and status than the victim. This kind of top-down power relationship occurs in supervisor-to-subordinate bullying. In situations of workplace bullying, 72% of the bullies are bosses,[3] leaving a minority of bullying carried out by others in the organization who are not bosses or supervisors.

As in workplace bullying, workplace mobbing can also occur in top-down power relationships where the perpetrators hold more power and status than the victims. However, the opposite also happens in mobbings. Those with lower power and status on the organizational chart can gang up and mob someone in the organization who has higher status and greater institutional power. In workplace mobbings, power is more fluid and flows among those who have ganged up in order to drive someone out of the organization, whether the target is of lower rank, the same rank, or higher rank.

In workplace mobbings, power is not associated with organizational rank or status alone. In the wake of workplace conflicts that trigger mobbings, power can shift rapidly among organizational subgroups regardless of how high or low those groups are within the organizational hierarchy. Coalition forming and shifts in organizational

TABLE 1.1   Comparing and Contrasting Workplace Bullying and Workplace Mobbing

	Scenario One: Workplace Bullying	Scenario Two: Workplace Mobbing
Victim	High performer	High performer with a reputation for speaking out
Perpetrators	Single individual (direct supervisor)	Multiple organizational members (supervisors, subordinates, and same level coworkers)
Organizational context	Responsive to complaint from employee about hostile work environment	Unresponsive to employee complaint; toxic organizational culture; unethical and abusive organizational leadership; unethical organizational communication; routine abuse of power and misuse of organizational investigatory and disciplinary channels
Triggering event	None other than routine assignment of employee to different department	Challenge by the employee to the status quo or "the way things are done around here"
Types of abusive acts	Relentless criticism of job performance; failure to acknowledge job skills and strengths; excessive job scrutiny and micromanagement; unreasonable work demands	Gossip; innuendo; character and personality attacks; improper and intrusive personnel investigation; defamation
Method of carrying out abusive acts	Direct perpetrator-to-victim interactions	Concerted actions, many covert, by multiple organizational members; designed to subject the victim to excess and unwarranted scrutiny and investigation; carried out through the use of both formal and informal procedures; unethical communication
Motivation and goals of perpetrator(s)	Exercise of power and control	Elimination of the victim from the organization and stripping the victim of respect, status, and influence

alliances can allow those lower in the hierarchy to hold greater power over those higher in the hierarchy and to successfully mob them.

For example, senior managers can be mobbed by junior managers and line staff. Professors can be mobbed by junior professors, staff, and students. Nurse managers can be mobbed by charge nurses and staff nurses. School principals can be mobbed by teachers and administrative staff.

Of course, the converse is also true. Senior managers, nurse managers, professors, and school principals can participate in the mobbing of those lower than them on the organizational chart. Mobbings can run in all directions in the hierarchy of the organization. A victim can be mobbed by supervisors, by those at the same organizational level, by subordinates on the organizational chart, by persons served by the organization, and, not infrequently, by a combination of participants who represent multiple levels of the organization.

No one wants a boss like Jim's in Scenario One—a micromanager who harangues and criticizes and is impossible to please. We can call her a bully if we wish, and we can certainly deduce that her personnel management skills are sorely lacking. However, unlike in mobbing, she does her bullying herself and does it directly to her victim.

In mobbing, the effort to strip victims of their respect, stature, and influence and to drive them from the organization is a joint activity carried out by multiple perpetrators and utilizes both formal and informal channels within the organization. The abusive acts are intended to humiliate and discredit a victim and are often focused on the victim's character, personality, and working style as much or more than on his or her job performance. Mobbing victims are routinely characterized as difficult to work with, as troublemakers, as not being team players, as bullies, and even as mentally unstable. Their personal and professional identities are globally attacked and maligned.

Organizational Procedures and Workplace Mobbings

As noted in mobbings, both formal and informal channels within the organization are used to humiliate and drive the victim out. Organizational meetings are convened under the cloak of secrecy and confidentiality to address the question of what to do about the target-victim. Openness and transparency are notably lacking, and meetings are held and decisions made without providing meaningful opportunities for the target-victim to learn what the complaints are and to respond. There is a collective ganging up on the mobbing target that is carefully orchestrated to provide the mobbers with maximum deniability that they are singling out a target. "We are just following organizational procedures," is their mantra. David Yamada, the author of the Healthy Workplace Bill, draft legislation designed to protect all employees from workplace abuse while also protecting organizations from frivolous lawsuits, advises that when a lot of people in the workplace are saying the same thing about someone else it is a telltale sign of workplace mob formation.[4] His advice is well worth heeding.

In addition to the use of formal organizational channels to mob a victim, informal organizational channels are also used. These channels make use of an organization's grapevine and other informal communication networks. Gossip, innuendo, mischaracterization, and misrepresentation of facts all travel rapidly through informal organizational channels. Such organizational networks and grapevines are very effective at distributing information that can strip a worker of dignity, respect, and stature.

Mobbing victims are scapegoats for larger organizational problems and conflict, the consequences of which are then blamed on the mobbing victim. Mobbing perpetrators justify themselves and their coordinated efforts to undermine a victim by pointing to organizational procedures and protocols, protection of the organization's interests, and the need for corrective action. Mobbers who choose to carry out a part of their abuse through the supervision and performance evaluation process often use insinuation and are sanctimonious and preachy in how they undermine and tear down their victim in the written evaluation. When all the fingers are pointing in the same direction at a target-victim, it is very difficult for the victim to get a fair hearing (or any hearing) or to prevail with an intact reputation.

Workplace Mobbing, Identity, and Career Trajectory

In the popular television series *Mad Men*, about a Madison Avenue advertising agency and set in the 1960s, Freddy Rumsen, a copywriter, says to his bosses after being fired, "If I don't go into that office every day, who am I?"[5] That line, laced with meaning, reverberates for anyone who has ever been fired and especially for anyone who has ever been forced out of a job as a result of workplace mobbing. For better or for worse, job, career, and personal identity are tightly interconnected and a rupture in one causes ruptures in the others.

Because workplace mobbing is associated not only with job loss but also with damage to one's personal and professional reputation, the identity injuries that mobbing victims suffer are often severe. Freddy Rumsen's question becomes a frightening refrain for mobbing victims because frequently they don't know the answer to it. We do, after all, locate ourselves and each other in the social world based in large part on our jobs and occupational identities. When someone loses a job involuntarily through workplace mobbing it's not just one's career, it's also one's personal identity and life course trajectory that get disturbed and tossed around.

No one wants to be mobbed. There is no possible secondary gain to be derived from it. The only thing mobbing brings is injury and hurt. People do not go to work expecting to be mobbed. Reasonable people expect work to have its share of ups and downs, good times and more difficult times. What employees don't expect and have never planned for is to be driven from their workplaces through a dirty-tricks campaign of emotional abuse. When mobbing happens it represents a significant and traumatic break in people's hopes, dreams, and plans for their work lives and their futures. People who have been mobbed at work and successfully driven from their workplaces through firing or quitting are often afraid of working again in organizations.

Our experience suggests that this fear of returning to organizational work life after being mobbed is a deep fear that alters the course of mobbing victims' careers and lives. Some mobbing victims end up working for themselves through a process of what career counselors call push-motivation[6] to self-employment and entrepreneurship. It's not that they were strongly attracted to self-employment or entrepreneurship; they felt pushed into it by their experiences of having been mobbed and fears of returning to organizational life. Other mobbing victims do return to organizational life, but they return changed and, at the very least, more wary of their work environments and coworkers. For some mobbing victims, the trauma of having been mobbed and its aftermath of destructive consequences leave them unable to return to work for the foreseeable future.

In Brief: Workplace Mobbing

"Workplace mobbing is nonsexual harassment of a coworker by a group of members of an organization for the purpose of removing the targeted individual(s) from the organization or at least a particular unit of the organization. Mobbing involves individual, group, and organizational dynamics. It predictably results in the humiliation, devaluation, discrediting, and degradation; loss of professional reputation; and, often, removal of the victim from the organization through termination, extended medical leave, or quitting. The results of this typically protracted traumatizing experience are significant financial, career, health, and psychosocial losses or other negative consequences."[7]

Who Is Likely to Get Mobbed?

Not everyone who works in an organization gets mobbed, so it's reasonable to ask whether a certain kind of personality type or profile is more likely to be targeted. Current research does not indicate that there is a typical psychological profile of a mobbing victim. People with all kinds of different personality types have been mobbed or bullied. No reliable pattern of psychological type has emerged to identify likely mobbing or bullying victims.

In the United States and in the Western world more generally, we tend to place blame on individuals rather than on groups or larger contexts when bad things happen. We routinely explain negative outcomes by looking for the bad apple in the barrel. We regularly hear comments like, "Someone is going to pay for this; someone must be held accountable." Our first and strongest impulse when looking for explanations of why something happened that we don't like is to focus on individually based explanations—especially on personality factors.

This impulse is so strong—and so erroneously biased—that social psychologists have a name for it. They call it the *fundamental attribution error*.[8,9] This bias or error describes how people commonly overemphasize individually based explanations for events and situations and underemphasize group, organizational, and contextual explanations. So when someone becomes a victim of workplace mobbing and loses his job by being fired or quitting, the fundamental attribution error leads people to explain what happened by looking for something wrong in the individual—most often in the victim who has been targeted and blamed by the organization—rather than by looking for problems at the organizational and contextual levels.

While research hasn't provided any sound psychological profiles of victims, some intriguing social and relational profiles of who is likely to be a target of workplace mobbing are beginning to emerge. Employees and workers who are more likely to become mobbing targets include those who are not organizational insiders and who deviate in important ways from the culture, structure, and leadership of their particular organizations. These profiles, therefore, do not identify fixed qualities of mobbing targets. Instead they describe relational qualities—qualities of personality and behavior that *in relation* to the organizational culture and structure mark an employee or worker as different and as an outsider. It is this outsider status and these differences from the organizational culture that increase the likelihood that certain employees and workers will be mobbed.

Employees/Workers More Likely to Be Mobbed

- Employees/workers who speak out or challenge organizational dynamics or organizational policies and procedures are more likely to be mobbed than employees who don't speak out.[7,10]
- Employees/workers who expose corruption and/or wrongdoing or who speak out in the public interest are more likely to be mobbed than those who do not.[10,11]
- Employees/workers who work for organizational and other kinds of change are more likely to be mobbed than those who do not.[10]
- Employees/workers who are outsiders and who are different from the cultural norm are more likely to be mobbed than those who are cultural insiders.

Such outsiders include those whose gender, race, and sexual identity are different from the dominant identities within the organization.[10,12] They also include immigrants and first-generation children of immigrants whose communicative styles and practices are different from the culturally and organizationally dominant communication styles.[13]

How Common Is Workplace Mobbing?

It would be nice to think that workplace mobbing is rare, but it is not. It happens with alarming frequency. Although different researchers use different methods for identifying prevalence rates of workplace abuse and different terminology in reporting those rates, the reported frequency of workplace abuse in the United States is consistently high. Workplace abuse researcher Pamela Lutgen-Sandvik and her colleagues concluded that "given the data available, we can speculate that approximately 35–50% of U.S. workers experience one negative act at least weekly in any 6–12 month period, and nearly 30% experience at least two types of negativity frequently."[14] The Workplace Bullying Institute/Zogby International U.S. Workplace Bullying Survey, the largest survey of its kind, found that 35% of American workers had experienced workplace abuse at some time in their working lives.[15]

Workplace abuse has already reached epidemic status as suggested by these statistics, and they only refer to the United States. In other countries, the situation is no better, with high rates of reported workplace abuse. For example, a study of health care workers in the United Kingdom[16] found that 37% of participants had experienced workplace abuse in the previous year and that a disturbing 96% of those had experienced abuse by more than one person. In Turkey, a recent study among nurses reported that a profoundly alarming 86% had experienced workplace mobbing behaviors in the previous 12-month period.[17] A workplace study in Taiwan identified a 1-year prevalence rate of 51% for verbal abuse and 16% for mobbing.[18] In France, mobbing is a crime referred to as "moral harassment" for which there are both civil and criminal penalties.

These kinds of frequency statistics from the United States and other countries around the world challenge anyone to consider workplace mobbing and other forms of workplace abuse as minor or insignificant problems. Workplace mobbing is sufficiently widespread and is accompanied by such serious health consequences that it rises to the level of a public health problem requiring public health awareness and action to resolve.

Conclusion

While workplace bullying and workplace mobbing have abusive behavior directed toward a target in common, they have important distinctive features. Workplace bullying involves an individual or a group of people behaving aggressively and abusively toward a victim, but the organization through the exercise of its leadership and authority is not involved as a coparticipant in it. In workplace bullying, the exercise of power and control over another provides the ignition for the aggressive and abusive behavior. In workplace mobbing, organizational leadership and other members support and participate in overt or covert actions designed to drive a victim from the workplace and strip the person of dignity, respect, and credibility.

Understanding the difference between workplace bullying and workplace mobbing is important because you can't solve workplace mobbing by only addressing the bullying behaviors of individuals. Since organizations are the incubators of workplace mobbing, solving the problem of mobbing requires awareness and change at the organizational level as well as at the individual level.

Based on the research that has been conducted, the frequency of workplace mobbing around the world is alarmingly and perhaps surprisingly high. The consequences of workplace mobbing are potentially so severe for victims that their careers and life courses are often changed forever, as we have discussed in this chapter. In later chapters we will discuss the damage to physical and psychological health inflicted by workplace mobbing and its impact on family members and family relationships.

Making workplaces mobbing-resistant and psychologically safe places for workers is the urgent next frontier for public health action. Workplace mobbing is not a problem that can be solved by telling targets and victims to toughen up and develop thicker skin or to just get over it and move on with their lives. Too many workers have been hurt by workplace mobbing already and have had their careers, health, family relationships, and lives permanently altered. Everyone must pay more attention, not less, to the problem of workplace mobbing in order to solve it.

Ganging Up in Workplaces

M OST PEOPLE HAVE TO WORK SO THAT THEY CAN
support themselves and their families and so that they can get
health insurance to provide care for themselves and their families if
someone gets sick. There aren't that many independently wealthy
people around who can just say "take this job and shove it" if things
aren't going well for them. Work is a basic need, and its threatened loss, especially as a result of mobbing, results in primal fear.
Workplace mobbing involves people ganging up on a target-victim in
a display of what has been referred to as the "eliminative impulse" in
formal organizations,[1] the lust to bring someone down and remove
him or her from the organization.

The concept of workplace mobbing was formulated and explained
by Heinz Leymann, a psychiatrist and industrial psychologist, who
spent his academic and research life studying the phenomenon in
Sweden. Not only did he do the scientific research necessary to understand the ganging up, aggression, and elimination central to workplace mobbing, but he also did considerable work caring for those
who had been injured as a result of it. Leymann was both a scholar
and a healer. In his recently translated book, *Workplace Mobbing
as Psychological Terrorism*,[2] Leymann emphasized the significance
of unethical communication in the development and acceleration of

workplace mobbing. Leymann saw unethical communication as both igniting workplace mobbing and as powering it once it got started.

Ganging up in workplaces against a target-victim cannot be done without multiple workers, administrators, and managers willing to participate in unethical communication that is both verbal and written. Among the forms of unethical communication that we identify are

- gossip
- lies
- rumors
- innuendo
- ridicule
- belittlement
- disparagement
- humiliation
- false information
- dissemination of such information
- failure to correct false information
- leaks of personal and confidential information
- not providing information necessary for a worker to complete the requirements of his or her job
- isolating a worker
- ignoring an employee
- giving an employee the "cold shoulder"
- excessive "writing up" of a worker by a supervisor or manager
- disciplinary action and reprimands without obtaining information from all parties
- inaccurate or abusive performance evaluations
- withholding of job references needed by a worker to obtain other work.

Without such unethical communication ganging up and mobbing could not happen. To understand the dynamics of ganging up in workplaces, let's start with a story.

Sacking the Football Coach

He was fit and attractive. They were quite a bit overweight, and their attractiveness or unattractiveness was a matter of opinion and talk after it was all over. He graduated from the high school where he became head football coach, but even that didn't make him an insider in the rural southwestern county where he had spent his adolescence and eventually returned to try and lead the football team to victory. His family was wealthy in a town where most people scrambled to stay in the middle class. After graduating from college he spent a few years coaching a semiprofessional football team in a different country. That meant he worked and lived outside of the country for a couple of years before returning to his high school alma mater to take the job as head football coach, and he brought back with him some "foreign" ways.

His alumni status notwithstanding, he was an outsider in a high school where key staff and faculty members had a penchant for carving up the world into insiders and outsiders. But Dwayne, as we'll call him, was a peculiar kind of outsider, one who also had some insider knowledge and experience since he had lived in the community for a while and had received his high school diploma there. Casual observers would have thought of Dwayne as an insider, but he wasn't. His background, his resources, his opportunities, his religion, his living abroad all made him very different from just about everyone else who worked at the high school and lived in the community. But like almost everyone at the school and in his town, Dwayne did love football and pretty much any and every sport that people either played or watched.

Dwayne was hired as the head football coach when there was a vacancy in the high school athletic department. He had tired of living abroad and wanted to return to the United States to raise his family. Returning to the small southwestern town where he had finished growing up before going on to college and where other family members still lived seemed like the idyllic thing to do. He had a lot of football coaching experience and brought new ideas, along with his experience, to his new job. Dwayne knew that the school and the town put a lot of money and energy into the football team and that they expected their team to win. The football team was young and unfocused, and had not been doing well.

Dwayne was confident he could turn the team around in a reasonable amount of time. He needed a rebuilding year before the team would be able to really take off and, having had those kinds of discussions with the school board, was given an initial contract that everyone involved could agree on. Dwayne was all set. He was excited about his new job and optimistic that he could turn the team around. He even hoped that with time and patience he could get the old-time assistant coaches—some of whom felt that the job of head coach should have been theirs—on board with the new program too.

But it didn't work out that way. Almost from the beginning and more likely from before Dwayne even led his football team onto the field for their first game, the fingers were pointing in a hostile way toward Dwayne. The assistant coaches who had wanted Dwayne's job but didn't get it complained that they didn't like his coaching style. They tried to make their generalized negative comments about Dwayne more specific and therefore more credible by adding that Dwayne designed plays that were too hard for the kids to learn. Dwayne thought that the plays were not above average in complexity and that, even if they were, the kids were more than capable of learning and implementing them. Not that it seemed to matter; the kids weren't complaining about the plays and from all indications seemed to like Dwayne well enough and certainly respected him as their coach.

The negative comments about Dwayne and the backbiting about his coaching style and playbook escalated fairly quickly. It didn't take long for the contentiousness within the athletic department to spread to the rest of the school and then beyond to the community at large. The high school's grapevine began to buzz about Dwayne and his coaching style. Rancor and animosity toward Dwayne seemed to materialize out of nowhere.

Some school employees, including teachers, started deliberately searching out any negative information they could find about Dwayne. Whatever they found was given a pejorative spin and sent out through the grapevine that was already electric with nastiness and gossip. Somebody came up with some negative information that they had found on the Internet about his business dealings with his foreign football team and sent that information out through emails and the school's grapevine.

The situation was out of control. The school's chief administrator, who had a reputation for fairness and thoughtfulness, did not defend Dwayne nor do anything to stop the wildfire of gossip and malice that had already spread about him. It seems like the administrator thought that the situation would just have to burn out and the chips fall where they may. He didn't do a thing to rein in what by the end amounted to hate speech about Dwayne. By this time the school was split, with some supporting Dwayne and some, a much more vocal group, plotting his termination. The community at large mirrored the high school, with some residents supporting Dwayne and a much more vocal group demanding his ouster.

In the end, which came midway through Dwayne's second year as head football coach, he was fired. The football team had not had a good season, so the administrators and coaches involved felt justified, even morally righteous, about their decision to formally terminate Dwayne. They had grounds. The football team had a losing season.

After news of Dwayne's firing spread, some of the coaches, teachers, and other school personnel who had ganged up against him went into his office without permission and started to pack it up. Given his travels and his lifelong love of sports, Dwayne had collected a lot of sports memorabilia and had some pieces that were special to him on display in his office. During the events following his firing, a piece of sports memorabilia that was important to Dwayne turned up missing, and he presumed it to be stolen.

Dwayne was outraged, certainly about his missing sports memorabilia, but now everything came to a head for him—all the feelings of bewilderment, violation, and betrayal that he had kept at bay for eighteen months surfaced. Word spread that Dwayne was on his way to the school to pick up his belongings and that he was furious. Some of the same group that had packed up Dwayne's office without his permission started telling the administrators to stop Dwayne from entering the building and to call the sheriff because Dwayne was potentially violent and a safety risk. Dwayne was angry all right, but he was certainly not violent.

After Dwayne was fired, staying in the idyllic little southwestern town where he went to high school no longer seemed like a good idea. He had his wife and kids to consider, and he wasn't sure whether he would ever be able to get over the bitterness of the last eighteen months. Besides, he wanted to coach football, and he had a life to live. Those who had mobbed Dwayne packed up his office for him. But Dwayne packed up his house himself and left town with his family. Dwayne was not only mobbed out of his job—he was also mobbed out of his hometown.

Pushed to the Brink

One of the final injuries during the active phase of Dwayne's mobbing came when the group boxed up his personal belongings, without authorization, after which a prized piece of sports memorabilia turned up missing. This provocative behavior on the part of the mobbing group understandably angered and riled Dwayne, whom the group then claimed was dangerous because he got angry. Such labeling of mobbing victims as "disturbed" or "unstable" after they have been egregiously provoked and then responded with anger or another emotion is classic in workplace mobbings. It is important that this kind of double bind that commonly occurs in workplace mobbings not be ignored but, instead, acknowledged and named.

In another workplace mobbing, an employee kept a cherished photo of a child on her office door. At some point in the mobbing of this woman, the photo was defaced, and she reported it both to company security and her supervisors. Her assistant manager responded both verbally and, later in writing, that it was hard to see the lines that were drawn and etched across the child's face—that the photo had only been defaced a little bit. Her supervisor went on to suggest that she was overreacting and paranoid.

Intensifying provocation of the victim is the point at which mobbings become very dangerous and potentially volatile, not just for the victim, but also for others in the workplace. In Dwayne's case, a flashpoint was reached when the group packed up his belongings and his prized sports memorabilia went missing. This was the point at which Dwayne became outraged. He was angry but never violent, even though he was characterized that way by those involved in the mobbing. Dwayne's emotional control and discipline kept a highly volatile situation from going from bad to worse.

When mobbing targets are vilified, humiliated, and otherwise provoked it is fairly easy to envision how some might respond aggressively and, on occasion, violently. Indeed, research suggests that individuals who are socially excluded or ostracized act more aggressively and participate less in behavior directed at caring about and helping others.[3,4] Under threat, humans and other animals respond by activation of the "fight, flight, or freeze" response.[5] Each type of response has consequences for the victim whose whole body is invoking it. But "fight" has potentially dangerous consequences for others as well. The ultimate "fight" response is homicide, the ultimate "flight" response is suicide, and the ultimate "freeze" response is sudden death. When the "fight" response is activated in mobbing victims who have been humiliated and provoked and who experience a life threat in the form of potential or actual job loss, the risk of violence increases. Mobbing victims are more likely to commit suicide[6,7] than they are to commit homicide, but the path to homicide can also be traced.

In Dwayne's case, he became very angry and yelled at a group of his coworkers whom he saw as coordinating the attacks on him, asking, "When is this going to stop?" He made no threats against any coworkers nor did he become physically violent toward them. Dwayne's anger and direct verbal confrontation of a group of his coworkers can be seen as a form of the "fight" response. Dwayne's anger manifested as raising his voice. However, it is not hard to imagine how the "fight" response in a situation similar to Dwayne's could end up in physical violence with the potential for injury to the mobbing victim, coworkers, or both.

Insiders and Outsiders and How They Get That Way

Context always determines who is an insider and who is an outsider. There are no absolute qualities, attributes, or characteristics that can be held up as indicative of outsider status. The determination of insider or outsider status has to be made based on the reference group in question. In Dwayne's case, his personal attractiveness, his financial resources, his religion, his having lived out of the country, and his different way of doing things made him an outsider in relation to the influential groups within his school and community. He was always held at arm's length in spite of his childhood ties to both the school and the community, and he was never part of the in-group.

It may be surprising that Dwayne, a white male with money and education, was not part of the dominant group in his small town. But he wasn't. He was wealthy, and those who were successful at his school were generally only a single generation up from poverty. Dwayne's religion also set him apart. He was mainline Presbyterian, and most of the staff at the high school, indeed within the whole community, were Baptist and attended church together. In a community with a high average obesity index, including the members of the high school athletic department, Dwayne also stood out because of his level of physical fitness and attractiveness. In terms of the broader culture, the differences that Dwayne represented may seem small and insignificant. But at Dwayne's high school, and within his small, rather insular town and community, these differences were more than enough to set him apart from the in-group. Once the process of ganging up on Dwayne to push him out began, the piling-on just didn't end. Because of his differences from the school and community insiders it was much easier to see Dwayne as "other" and to get rid of him.

Difference Is a Relative Concept

Anyone can be ganged up on and mobbed. Being different can increase the risk of victimization as a result of workplace mobbing. Difference includes but is not limited to minority status in terms of gender, race, religion, ethnicity, social class, sexual orientation, age, national origin, immigration status, and so on. Difference can only be understood in relation to a particular group, organization, or culture—as "difference from" the group, organization, or culture in question. Difference is a relative term. In one context a person can be of minority status based on a particular attribute or set of attributes. The same person can be of majority status in a different context.

Within workplaces, whether a worker questions policies and procedures or readily accepts and adapts to them, speaks out or remains quiet, prefers to work alone or with others, takes the initiative or waits and follows orders, is introverted or extroverted are examples of attributes and working styles that can either keep a worker in the mainstream of his or her particular organization or set him or her apart. It just depends on the organization's culture and its tolerance or lack of tolerance for divergent ways of thinking and behaving.

Being different from the existing in-group within an organization or community, on any number of characteristics or dimensions, is likely to increase the risk of being mobbed. In some workplaces and organizations, characteristics that are dominant in the wider society are minority characteristics within the particular organization. Difference is always relative. Figure 2.1 presents another perspective on the relationship between difference and context.

```
                     why i was mobbed⁸

because i ask too many questions

because i am loyal

because i have opinions

because I push his/her buttons

because i have ideas

because i am encumbered whatever that means

because i am old

because i am young

because i disagree

because i speak up

because i am gay

because i am straight

because i get things done

because i am an immigrant

because i don't always go along to get along

because i don't get the organizational culture

because i am a child of immigrants

because the organizational culture isn't my culture

because i am not a team player

because i don't get what it means to be a team player
```

FIGURE 2.1 "why I was mobbed" (*Continued*)

```
because I am a woman

because I am a man

because i say what is wrong

because i say what is right

because i cost too much

because i am independent

because I laugh too loudly

because i keep to myself

because i talk too much

because i don't talk enough

because i am a person of color

because i am not a person of color

because i am smart

because i am slow

because i don't dress right

because i don't look right

because i'm religious

because i'm an atheist

because i have a vision

because i don't have a vision

because I did too little

because I did too much
```

FIGURE 2.1 (*Continued*)

Workplace Conflict Out of Control

In workplaces and in organizational life in general, conflict is expectable. It is the flip side of the coin to cooperation. The presence of conflict in a workplace or within a unit of a workplace is no more unusual than is the presence of cooperation. People in workplaces regularly pull together in impressive displays of cooperation to accomplish a task or meet an important deadline for an organizational project. Just as regularly, people in workplaces disagree with one another about a project's goals or about the best strategies to achieve those goals. They have personality conflicts and differences of opinions. Such conflict is about as common and as routine as workplace cooperation.

Relationships, be they workplace, social, or familial, don't exist without good measures of both cooperation and conflict. Mobbing happens when conflicts in a workplace (1) escalate out of control, (2) begin to involve increasing numbers of people, (3) are left without effective intervention by management, (4) result in the targeting of a victim for blame (otherwise known as scapegoating) who is then held responsible for both starting and stopping the conflict and who, ultimately, is eliminated from the organization.

In the case of Dwayne, the ostensible conflict was over differences of opinion among the assistant coaches about his coaching style and the complexity of the football plays in his playbook. The focus of the conflict quickly shifted from the issues of coaching style and the appropriate level of complexity of football plays for high school students to wholesale attacks on Dwayne as a person and on his personal history. Unethical communication in the form of gossip and assaults on Dwayne's integrity and character escalated rapidly and, at times, rose to the level of hate speech. Wholesale condemnations like "no one here really likes him," "he's not good for the program," "he doesn't fit in and he never has," "if he doesn't leave the other football coaches will," "we've got to make it so miserable for him that he does leave—he's got the money so it's not really a big deal" were spread around with little to no restraint. Many in the school community saw what was happening and were appalled but did not stand up for Dwayne. The principal, who ordinarily would not have tolerated the level of verbal abuse and personal attacks that were directed toward Dwayne, did not intervene. Even after the unauthorized entry into Dwayne's office and his sports memorabilia turned up missing, the principal did not investigate or discipline anyone.

In Dwayne's case, the conflict that triggered his mobbing and snowballed to the size that it did actually started before Dwayne ever showed up on the job. Several assistant football coaches believed that they should have been offered the head football coaching position and that they were better candidates than Dwayne. They were resentful from the moment the deal was sealed with Dwayne. Not only did they not help Dwayne with his efforts to rebuild the football team, but they also actively undermined him any chance they could. They kept Dwayne at arm's length and reminded him at every opportunity that he was the outsider and they were the insiders.

In other situations of ganging up leading to mobbing, a workplace conflict or dispute emerges that is not resolved, and it festers. It is a kind of conflict that goes beyond the normal and expectable conflicts of everyday work life. Let's consider an example. Members of a work unit have strongly held beliefs about what are the best strategies for achieving their goals, but the work unit is more or less divided into two factions, with one group believing that one set of strategies must be utilized and the other group believing that a different set of strategies must be utilized. Obviously, the work unit can't endorse two competing sets of strategies, so ultimately one group's strategies are selected.

In this case, the group that didn't get its way was unwilling to accept the decision. So this group took matters into its own hands. It started the ganging up process on the work unit leader and on some of the members of the group who held different ideas from them by resorting to unethical communication, including wholesale embellishment of the facts, outright lies, gossip, slander, and the holding of secret meetings to which only those "on their side" were invited. The leader of the group participating in abusive behavior and mobbing would make comments like "we are going to take him down" and "we will not stop until our goal is accomplished." Contrary to all company policy, the leader of the unsuccessful and discontented faction successfully induced high-ranking members of the organization to attend the secret meetings that were held off company property. The secretiveness, deception, and lack of transparency of the tactics used by this group were mind-boggling. But this group was tenacious as well as abusive and was successful in recruiting key supervisors to join them in undermining the work unit leader. They successfully waged a mobbing that was like a coup.

The kind of conflict that emerges around a contentious workplace issue and devolves into ganging up and mobbing is particularly interesting. It's often in this kind of organizational conflict that traditional understandings of power as being held by those with high organizational rank and status must give way to newer understandings of power as fluid and shifting among groups of any rank or status depending upon the specifics of the situation. In this example,

Seven Warning Signs That Workplace Conflict Could Become Mobbing

- Management pathologizes (views as abnormal) the general experience of workplace conflict instead of seeing it as normal and expectable.
- When there is a conflict, the focus shifts away from the issues and toward the person or people involved.[1]
- Unethical communication in the form of gossip, defamation, character attacks, and other kinds of verbal abuse escalates and is distributed throughout the organization.[2]
- Bystanders in the workplace do not stand up for a victim of workplace abuse and mobbing nor do they introduce more accurate narratives about the victim, thus allowing the destructive narrative to continue to circulate.
- In the presence of an escalating conflict, management fails to intervene effectively to resolve the conflict.[2]
- Management blames the victim for the initiation of the conflict.
- Management places the responsibility for solving the conflict on the victim and blames the victim for failing to solve it.

an unresolved conflict escalated and spiraled out of control, and the employee who was successfully ganged up on and mobbed was of higher organizational rank than those initiating the abusive behavior against him.

How Management Participates in Ganging Up

Let's return to the case of Dwayne to look at how management participated in ganging up on him. Those involved in ganging up and mobbing Dwayne were on a mission. They had an agenda to get rid of him and were purposeful and motivated in seeing it through. Some teachers and other school personnel lustily participated with the assistant football coaches in tracking down any negative information they could about Dwayne and spreading it around. This group was out in the open about its activities and its intent to have Dwayne removed as the head football coach. Anyone in the school or community who knew what this group was up to also knew what their endgame was. But the principal, the chief executive of the high school and the county school system's major representative, participated in ganging up on Dwayne in a very different way. The principal who had a reputation for fairness and thoughtfulness participated in ganging up on Dwayne by doing nothing. He stood by and let the flagrantly unethical and destructive information about Dwayne spread throughout the school community without lifting a finger to oppose it or otherwise stop it.

Very likely, the principal was caught up in his own political dilemmas about Dwayne's situation. After all, it was the principal who had given the final approval to hire him as the head football coach. But he had also heard school district administrators, some of whom had kids on the football team, speak disparagingly of Dwayne after school board meetings and mimic Dwayne's accent and other "airs and graces" that they believed he affected as a result of the time he spent living out of the country. The principal didn't want any trouble with his own job, and he certainly didn't want to be dragged into the mess that was Dwayne's situation. So he took the course of least resistance and let the abuse go on, hoping it would not take long for it to burn out. Like others, the principal rationalized his own actions or, more accurately, his failure to act, because Dwayne had independent financial resources and would not be out in the cold. The assistant football coaches, teachers, and other school personnel participated openly and actively in the ganging up on Dwayne. The principal, and indeed higher county level administrators, participated just as aggressively through their failure to act to stop the abuse of Dwayne. The principal's aggressive acts were acts of omission.

The Process of Ganging Up

Workplace Conflict

- Long-standing or emergent
- Escalation of conflict
- No effective intervention by management

People Take Sides

- Target-victim or scapegoat is identified
- Number of people involved in conflict increases, including coworkers and other staff
- Ganging up accelerates
- Number of bystanders increases

Unethical Communication

- Gossip
- Rumors
- False information
- Failure to correct false information
- Ridicule, belittling, and humiliation
- Leaks of personal, confidential information
- Failure to stop dissemination of unethical communication
- Isolation and/or ignoring of target-victim
- "Cold-shoulder"
- Target-victim shut out of workplace information loops
- Secret meetings
- Escalation of unethical communication

Other Aggressive and Abusive Acts

- Vandalism or theft of target-victim's personal property
- Relocating of target-victim's office or work station away from work group

Involvement of Management or Administration

- Blaming the target-victim
- Holding the target-victim responsible for solving the conflict
- Unreasonable and excessive demands for increased work product
- Increased discipline and "writing up" of target-victim
- Inaccurate or abusive performance evaluations
- Purposeful development of "paper trail"
- Labeling the target-victim as "unstable," "discontented," or as a "troublemaker"
- Unwilling to consider alternative perspectives about the conflict, situation, and/or the target-victim

Elimination of the Target from the Workplace

- Fired
- Leaves voluntarily because can't take it anymore
- Becomes ill
- Goes on extended medical leave

Post-Elimination Unethical Communication

- Self-righteous justification of actions
- Celebration of target-victim's departure
- Continued disparagement of target-victim
- Withholding of a job reference critical for target-victim in search for other work

Why Not Just Get Rid of the Bully?

At first glance, it may look like the sensible thing to do is to just get rid of the bully. Who needs bullies who only end up causing harm to other workers and, in the end, to the organization as a whole? The problem is that, in workplace mobbing, the bully isn't a single individual, but a group of workers along with management or administrative involvement. Let's take a look at Dwayne's situation one more time. The assistant football coaches got the mobbing started by carping about Dwayne's coaching style and complaining that his playbook for the high school kids contained plays that were too complicated and too hard for the kids to remember and execute.

It wasn't long, though, before teachers and other staff members were actively involved with the assistant football coaches in trying to paint Dwayne as an incompetent coach, not a team player, and as a person of questionable character who should be removed from his position. The core group responsible for orchestrating the mobbing of Dwayne numbered between eight and ten. And that number doesn't include the principal and county school administrators who knew the kind of abuse to which Dwayne was being subjected and who stood by and did nothing. The problem of just going after the bully is both a practical one and a theoretical one.

On the practical side, even if it were possible, finding out just how many workers were actively involved in a mobbing is not an easy task. Workers join in a mobbing at various times during the process. Some participants are more visible and vocal than others who are not out front in a mobbing but who inflict harm nonetheless. Uncovering the "who," "what," and "when" of multiple participants' involvement in mobbing is difficult, to say the least. A few may even realize the harm they are inflicting by their involvement or learn that a lot of the information that is being communicated about a victim is false and out of context and decide to have no more part in the process. But that doesn't negate the harm that he or she did as a participant at an earlier stage of the mobbing. Going after all of the participants in a mobbing to discipline or remove them from an organization, even if it were possible, would be highly disruptive for any organization.

On the theoretical side, going "bully-hunting" doesn't make sense. While workplace mobbing does involve individual workers acting abusively, they are acting as a group, and it is this group and the wider organizational culture that allows mobbing to occur in the first place. Unhealthy and toxic organizational culture and leadership combine to create mobbing-prone organizations. Singling out an individual "bully" to blame and purge from the organization is generally a poor and wrong-headed solution to what is an organizational and not an individual problem. While it is very attractive for mobbing-prone organizations to go after individual "bullies" when there have been instances of workplace mobbing and other forms of abuse, the problem with such "bully-hunting" is that it allows the organization to sidestep the more important and serious responsibility of examining its own role when a mobbing occurs.

Conclusion

Ganging up and unethical communication are activities central to workplace mobbing. Ganging up on someone in the workplace with the end goal of eliminating him or her represents the dark side of social cohesion—working together to bring someone down. Ganging up always involves the marking off of people into in-groups and out-groups, insiders and outsiders. Mobs and gangs have long been justifiably feared. Targeting a worker for removal from the workplace requires that the target increasingly be seen as an outsider, as an "other" in order for the mob to be able to do its work of elimination. In most human and animal groups eliminating one of your own is extremely difficult. Workplace mobbing, therefore, requires the transforming of the target into an "other," into someone who is not one of your own and, therefore, much easier to get rid of.

In addition to multiple acts of proactive unethical communication, the ganging up and mobbing process also includes a form of unethical communication characterized by failure to act or silence in the face of worker mistreatment. These kinds of aggressive acts against a victim include acts of omission that involve failure to take action when action is called for. Such aggressive acts of omission are frequently committed by management and administration in their efforts to appear uninvolved in an escalating conflict that results in the mobbing of a victim. How groups, management, and administration play essential roles in workplace mobbing was our focus in this chapter. How organizations can become incubators for workplace mobbing is the focus of our next chapter.

How Mobbing Happens

W HAT CAUSES WORKPLACE MOBBING? IS IT BAD luck? Personality defects? Bad coworkers? Bad situations? Or, is it something else? As we indicated earlier, the mass media tends to portray mobbing as caused by individual dynamics, that is, the character defects or personal problems of the perpetrators of mobbing. This is the individual psychology explanation, and it contrasts sharply with the organizational psychology explanation. The organizational psychology explanation holds that mobbing is caused by three factors: individual dynamics *plus* group dynamics *plus* organizational dynamics. Not just one factor, but all three factors. Remember that you can think of dynamics as influencing or motivating characteristics or as the interplay of various characteristics within a person, group, or organization and between a person, group, and organization.

While useful, the individual dynamics explanation actually makes the situation worse because it fosters the *fundamental error of attribution*. Previously we described the fundamental attribution error as a way of explaining or attributing the cause of most problematic behaviors and misconduct as the result of individual dynamics, particularly an individual's psychological problems. Problematic behavior is seldom, if ever, attributed to group dynamics or organizational dynamics. From the individual dynamics explanation, mobbing is the result of a "bad apple," that is, either the mobber's or the victim's individual personality dynamics. Because it is so common, the "bad apple" explanation effectively trumps the "bad apples" explanation (group dynamics) and the "bad barrel" explanation (organizational dynamics), even when the latter explanations better account for problematic behavior and misconduct.

In other words, when it comes to explaining mobbing, its causes and its impact, the individual dynamics explanation is woefully insufficient. This chapter offers an explanation of the causes and antecedents of mobbing that incorporates individual dynamics, group dynamics, and organizational dynamics together. It describes and illustrates the interaction of these three sets of causes in what provides a comprehensive and compelling explanation for mobbing.

Causes of Mobbing: Individual, Group, and Organizational Dynamics

Research and professional practice consistently show that workplace mobbing is best understood as caused by a combination of individual dynamics, work group dynamics, and organizational dynamics.[1] This section describes all three.

Individual Dynamics

Many Americans and other Westerners commonly accept the "bad apple" explanation or hold the individual dynamics view of behavior, and so they are likely to attribute workplace mobbing and bullying to personality, psychological problems, or other individual factors. Three such factors—personality, work orientation, and coping styles—are described in this section.

PERSONALITY

An employee's personality and level of psychological maturity interact with the organization's dynamics and differentially influence that employee's response to abusiveness.[2] Some targets of workplace abuse experience greater or lesser health consequences than do others. Some victims are more vulnerable to the consequences of mobbing and bullying than others, and many hoped that understanding the personality structure of a victim would be useful. So far there has been scant research addressing the personality of mobbing victims. In fact, there has been relatively little research on personality and its relationship to mobbing and bullying.

What we know is that at least three different psychological profiles of victims have been identified after the experience of mobbing or bullying.[3] One profile involves a range of severe psychological problems and personality disturbances, for instance depression, anxiety, suspicion, uncertainty, and confusion. A second profile is characterized by depression and suspiciousness, while the third profile reflects a quite normal personality, despite having experienced mobbing. It is likely that specific vulnerabilities and hardiness factors exist among some victims. Those with psychological problems, low self-confidence, and high anxiety seem to be more likely to feel bullied and harassed and find it difficult to defend themselves from such behavior. At the present time, little is known about individuals who are most resilient to the effects of mobbing and bullying or those most likely to experience severe health consequences.

Similarly, little is known about the psychological profile of those who are most likely to perpetrate mobbing. Some research suggests that bullies are high on aggressiveness and social anxiety and low on social competence.[4] Other studies suggest that most bullies are narcissistic and egocentric.[5]

WORK ORIENTATION

A promising individual dynamic that may explain why some victims are more vulnerable to the consequences of mobbing and bullying is work orientation. Work orientation refers to an individual's attitude toward work. An attitude is reflected in an individual's thoughts, feelings, and behaviors. Three work orientations have been identified: job, career, and calling.[6] Those with a *job orientation* view their work as simply a job. For them, work is a means to a financial end so they can engage in nonwork activities like hobbies and other interests. Those with a *career orientation* value pay, prestige, promotion, and status, which are the main focuses of their work because they lead to higher self-esteem, increased power, and higher social standing. For individuals with a career orientation, personal identity is closely tied to their career and their work. For

Work Orientations[6]

Job

Focus: nonwork life
Value: work provides financial means to enjoy nonwork activities ("I work so I can play")
Fulfillment: interest and ambitions expressed off the job, such as in hobbies and other pastimes

Career

Focus: career advancement and promotion
Values: status, prestige, reputation, power, and wealth ("I work to get ahead")
Fulfillment: advancement, increased self-esteem, power, and social standing

Vocation/Calling

Focus: sense of meaning and serving others; making a difference
Values: passion, personal meaning, and serving trump money and status ("My work is my play")
Fulfillment: meaning, life/work satisfaction, sense of well-being, balance, and wholeness

many professionals, professional identity becomes personal identity. For those with a *calling orientation*, work is their passion, and they value the sense of fulfillment it provides them, while at the same time contributing to making the world a better place. The chart above provides additional information on these three work orientations.

In our experience, victims with a career orientation frequently experience more distress and disability than those with other work orientations. Because their personal-professional identity is so closely tied to their work, victims with career orientations often view the abusive attacks of others and particularly the threat of or actual job loss as an invalidation of their personal-professional identity.

Coping Style

Certain coping styles can successfully buffer the effects of stress. A common observation is that stress predicts poor health, while religious or spiritual involvement predicts good health. Among the various coping styles that buffer or reduce stress are religious coping styles. Recent dissertation research by one of our doctoral students (LS) showed that individuals who utilized a Surrender style of coping and who were the targets of workplace mobbing experienced considerably less emotional exhaustion and cynicism than the other three religious coping styles studied.[7] In the Surrender coping style, the individual experiences less stress because he or she believes that someone (i.e., God) is capable of overseeing negative situations that the individual views as beyond his or her control. In contrast, those who utilized a Self-Directing style were most likely to experience health problems and burnout following the experience of mobbing. In the Self-Directing coping style the individual believes that he or she is responsible for solving problems while God is passive. We point out that this research only involved pastors who reported being mobbed by members of their own congregations, so these findings may not apply to other work settings. Nevertheless, the Surrender coping style may be a protective factor for some mobbing victims that can significantly buffer their experience of the stress of mobbing.

Work Group Dynamics

In contrast to an individual dynamics perspective, the organizational psychology perspective considers group and situational dynamics of equal or greater importance in understanding behaviors. In the workplace, a group or team of individuals typically behaves as a unit or as an "in-group" because of group cohesiveness. When the forces of cohesion fail, the group begins to disintegrate and ceases to be a group. Group pride is a powerful cohesive force, and to the extent members feel proud of their group, so the group feels proud of itself. The creation of an "enemy" or an "other" can effectively increase group cohesiveness, which can contribute to our understanding of why members of a work group or team may engage in mobbing.

Groups of workers may be members of formal work teams or individuals may gather together in informal groups that coalesce around a specific workplace concern or an outside activity. Chance meetings at the coffee machine, impromptu lunch meetings, and informal telephone calls may lead to a plan to mob someone who has been dubbed a "problem" that needs to be neutralized, marginalized, or excluded from the organization.

Organizational Dynamics

While clinicians and psychotherapists tend to favor an individual dynamics explanation for workplace mobbing, organizational consultants should favor organizational dynamics explanations, although organizational consultants themselves can be biased in favor of individual explanations even when organizational explanations are more comprehensive and compelling. Organizational dynamics refer to the interplay of influences among an organization's subsystems, including its structure, culture, strategy, leaders, and members. Depending upon how these organizational dynamics operate, a particular organization can be mobbing-prone or mobbing-resistant or somewhere in-between. Organizational dynamics can provide a useful marker in assessing the likelihood that bullying and mobbing will occur within a given organization. But while organizational dynamics may be a necessary condition for workplace mobbing and bullying, they are not a sufficient condition. In other words, being employed in an organization with a mobbing- or bully-prone strategy, structure, culture, and leadership does not mean that such abusive behavior will inevitably occur; only that it is more likely to occur.

To help you better appreciate the influence of organizational dynamics, visualize your organization (or any other) as a set of five overlapping, concentric circles, where each circle represents subsystems of that organization—namely, structure, culture, strategy, leaders, and members/workers within a larger circle representing the organization's external environment. It is important to realize that each of these subsystems has the potential to either foster or prevent abusive actions such as mobbing. Figure 3.1 represents these interacting subsystems of organizations.

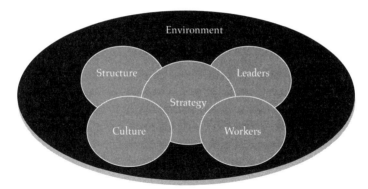

FIGURE 3.1 Organizational Subsystems.

STRATEGY

Strategy is the organization's overall plan or course of action for achieving its mission and goals. Strategy reflects the *actual* core values of the organization, which may or may not coincide with its *stated* core values. When the strategy of an organization emphasizes productivity and competitiveness at the expense of the well-being and job security of employees, such a strategy can foster workplace mobbing.

STRUCTURE

Structure is the organization's mechanisms for implementing its strategy. Structure includes policies, procedures, and reward and sanction systems. The organizational chart identifies the hierarchical levels within the organization and the reporting relationships of its members, employees and managers. Certain types of abusiveness are more likely to occur at particular levels of an organization. For example, attacks on professional abilities, involuntary job transfers, and dismissals are common in middle and upper levels of the organization.

CULTURE

Culture is the constellation of shared experiences, beliefs, assumptions, stories, customs, and actions that characterize the organization. Culture defines the organization's personality and identity to those inside and outside the organization. For abusiveness to occur within an organization aggressive elements must exist within a culture that permits and rewards it. A particular organization's culture may be sufficiently offensive, intimidating, or hostile that it interferes with the ability of certain workers to perform their jobs effectively.

LEADERS

Leadership involves inspiring, guiding, and coordinating others to achieve the organization's strategy and goals. Effective leadership maximizes its structure and resources, particularly personnel, in meeting its strategy and goals. Abusiveness in the work setting can involve varying levels of participation by management. Supervisors may look the other way or fail to discipline perpetrators, or they may participate in or initiate abusive behavior.

WORKERS

Workers and work teams collaborate with their leaders to accomplish the organization's mission and goals. Workers function best when leadership is responsive to and supportive of personnel needs and expectations. By contrast, a poor match between workers and leaders can lead to increased conflict, decreased productivity, and workplace abusiveness.

EXTERNAL ENVIRONMENT

External environment refers to factors outside the organization's internal dynamics that exert significant influence on the organization's strategy and functioning. These elements external to the internal dynamics of the organization include shareholders, competitors, customer demands, community, government regulations, and federal statutes. Such factors can either promote or hinder mobbing and other forms of interpersonal abuse and violence. For example, federal statutes regarding sexual harassment can reduce the incidence of that form of interpersonal abuse.

The following chart summarizes these subsystems.

Strategy	The organization's overall plan or course of action for achieving its mission and goals.
Structure	The organization's reporting relationships, policies and procedures, reward and sanction systems, and so on for achieving its strategy.
Culture	The organization's identity and personality; its unique beliefs, assumptions, stories, shared experiences, customs, and rituals that define the organization.
Leadership	The organization's way of focusing, guiding, inspiring, and coordinating personnel to achieve its strategy and goals.
Workers	The organization's workers and work teams who, in relationship with leadership, accomplish the organization's mission.
Environment	The organization's external factors: competitors, customer demands, community, and government regulations that influence and interact with it.

The Life Cycle of Organizations

Organizational dynamics provide a cross-sectional view of an organization but reveal little about an organization's developmental history over time, which is also referred to as the longitudinal view. Just as a person grows and develops and then declines, organizations also have life cycles. This life cycle of growth and decline has six stages.[8] These life cycle stages are helpful in understanding the development of mobbing. There are periods in organizations' growth and development in which, during times of expansion, transition, and decline related to increasing external threats, the organization is more likely to create conditions that give rise to the emergence of mobbing.

STAGE 1: NEW VENTURE

The critical tasks at this stage include defining a target group (for example, teens or computer users) and developing a product or service that targets such a group. In our service-driven economy the "products" provided in business ventures are often services like education, health care, social welfare, hospitality, religious ministry, and so on. Accomplishing these tasks requires the ability to extend or create a market need and the willingness to make a risky investment of time, energy, and money to create an organization that satisfies the identified unmet need. The abilities needed to accomplish these tasks are characteristic of the entrepreneurial leader, and the entrepreneurial leadership style is most compatible with this stage.

STAGE II: EXPANSION

Stage II is characterized by rapid growth and begins after the organization has been in stage I for a period of time. The major problems that occur in stage II involve growth rather than survival. Organizational resources are stretched to their limits as a new wave of members joins the organization, as demands for services increase, and as the organization's original, often primitive, day-to-day operating system becomes overwhelmed. Organizational "growing pains" are uncomfortably present. Growing pains signal that changes are needed and imply that the organization has not been totally successful in developing the internal system it needs for its rapid stage of growth.

STAGE III: PROFESSIONALIZATION

Stages I and II represent the entrepreneurial organization that often lacks well-defined goals, policies, plans, or controls. Even without these structures, the organizations prospered. As organizations outgrow their initial structures and operating systems, new structures and operating systems must be implemented. A new generation of workers with defined roles and responsibilities, performance standards, and control systems is usually needed to implement more formal planning.

STAGE IV: CONSOLIDATION

After transitioning to a professionally managed system, the organization can focus its efforts on consolidation. Consolidation means maintaining a reasonable increase in growth while developing the organizational culture. Culture becomes a critical concern in stage IV since current members may no longer share the organization's original core values, mission, and vision of what the organization is or where it is going. At stage IV, individual workers who are able to function interdependently with superiors, coworkers, and subordinates will be more compatible with the organization's collaborative or participative styles.

STAGE V: EARLY BUREAUCRATIZATION

Decline is an obvious indicator of bureaucratization. Status seeking, "business as usual," and appearances characterize the behavior of members as do internal turf wars. Negativity threatens to poison the organization's climate. The best and brightest start leaving the organization. The emphasis has clearly shifted from growth and maintenance to decline. Leadership is marked by administration and, in the later part of this stage, by inefficient administration. Passive-aggressivity becomes commonplace, reflecting demoralization among workers as well as among managers.

STAGE VI: LATE BUREAUCRATIZATION

During this stage miscommunication and lack of coordination and follow-through are common. The organizational culture reflects a sense of helplessness and a lack of common direction. It fosters attitudes like "come late, leave early," "do as little as you have to," "don't try to change anything," "protect job security at all costs." Leaders at this stage seem to be able to do little more than "keep the lights on." The eventual demise of the organization seems inevitable. Avoiding organizational decline associated with the negative features of early and late bureaucratization requires that organizations continuously evaluate their subsystems in relation to their external environment and mission and make necessary changes. The following chart summarizes these stages.

Some will find it helpful to visualize these stages in terms of a bell curve as indicated in Figure 3.2. Starting from the left, the curve accelerates or "grows" in the Expansion and Professionalization stages and tops out at the Consolidation stage. Then it decelerates or "declines" in the Early and Late Bureaucratization stages.

New Venture	The organization is launched to meet an unmet need. Tasks at this stage are to define a target market, develop a product or service targeted to it, and inspire worker effort and loyalty.
Expansion	The organization needs to develop basic operating systems and infrastructure that foster efficiency and effectiveness and to deal with role stress, high turnover, and so on.
Professionalization	The organization needs to implement a strategic management system and shift from entrepreneurial leadership that was effective for earlier stages to professional leadership.
Consolidation	The organization needs to maintain growth and worker and customer commitment, develop a consistent, healthy corporate culture, emphasize product or service quality, and avoid risky expansion.
Early Bureaucratization	The organization needs to maintain operating systems amid inefficiency, demoralization, passive-aggressivity, and loss of talented personnel.
Late Bureaucratization	The organization, unless major changes occur, is in terminal decline and can only be maintained by external life support systems.

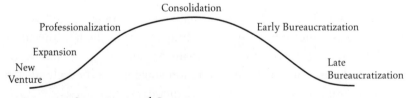

FIGURE 3.2 Organizational Stages.

Case of Thomas McIlvane and the U.S. Postal Service

This case, also analyzed and profiled in our previous book,[9] illustrates how individual, group, and organizational dynamics—particularly subsystems and organizational stage—interact to foster workplace abuse that profoundly impacts its victims.

The pejorative phrase "going postal" refers to shooting sprees in the workplace carried out by disaffected employees. A series of homicides that involved employees of the U.S. Postal Service (USPS) occurred between 1985 and 2006. One well-publicized incident occurred in Royal Oak, Michigan, at the regional postal sorting center. There a recently fired postal worker, Thomas McIlvane, killed four postal service managers, injured other postal workers who had been involved in his termination, and then committed suicide. Most subsequent official and press reports explained the murder and mayhem at Royal Oak exclusively on Thomas McIlvane's prior history of personal and psychological problems.[10] More recent reviews[11] of the deadly Royal Oak shootings and a new film[12] take a much broader look at the working conditions, manager-employee relationships, and workplace abuse of McIlvane and offer a much more nuanced picture of the events leading up to his murderous rage. Given these more recent analyses together with our own that follows, it is not far-fetched to conclude that Thomas McIlvane was a victim of workplace mobbing. Considering whether McIlvane was in fact mobbed at work is important for the prevention of similar tragedies in the future so that prevention can be implemented at the group and organizational levels as well as at the individual level. The following analysis is based on the individual, group, and organizational dynamics documented to exist at the time of the Royal Oak shooting.

Individual Dynamics

McIlvane, like other postal workers involved in shootings, was under severe job-related stress and had lost his job.[10] A former marine and champion kickboxer with a black belt in karate, he had been fired a year before the shooting for cursing at his supervisor as well as for threatening other clerks and fighting with customers. He had several times threatened violence if he was not reinstated. He appealed the dismissal through a union grievance procedure but lost an arbitration hearing prior to the shootings.

Work Group Dynamics

The operative group dynamic involved at the Royal Oak postal center was in-group versus out-group. Extreme negativity and long-standing tension characterized relationships between the management group and workers. Workers felt they were being treated inhumanely by their supervisors. Resentment toward management was so intense that after the shootings it was reported that postal workers had defaced the names of two dead managers on the memorial that was erected outside the building.[10] Coworkers of McIlvane's have since claimed that he was subject to workplace harassment and accused of violating rules that were commonly violated by postal workers but in his case were used as a basis for firing him.[12]

Organizational Dynamics

STRATEGY

The motto of the USPS is, "Neither snow nor rain nor heat nor gloom of night stays these couriers from the swift completion of their appointed rounds." Core values of loyalty, caring, reliability, and fast service are reflected in this motto. It is ironic that loyalty and caring seemed absent in management–worker relations, while management's demand for fast service from workers appears to have been unrelenting. As a government agency the USPS had adopted antidiscrimination and anti–sexual harassment policies and, had they been required, would also have adopted antimobbing and other anti-harassment policies.

STRUCTURE

The USPS has a disciplined, hierarchical, and bureaucratic organizational structure. High-speed sorting machines had replaced many workers at the Royal Oak center, but instead of layoffs management found various other ways of reducing the workforce with harsh discipline and measures that fostered high job strain.

Managers amplified minor worker infractions and turned them into major issues in order to justify firing that worker. The result was increased verbal altercations and violent assaults on managers by postal employees.[10]

CULTURE

This strategy and structure may explain the toxic climate filled with tension, distrust, and animosity between managers and workers. As in other high job strain organizations with high negativity toward managers, an abuse-prone culture is probable.

LEADERSHIP

The dominant management style is authoritarian, rigid, and militaristic. A large-scale, third-party study of the entire postal service documented this leadership style.[13]

WORKERS

Postal workers experienced high levels of job strain and animosity toward their managers. The result was that workers who were distressed externalized their frustration and acted out in fights, as in the case of McIlvane, or internalized it, contributing to medical and psychiatric disabilities.

EXTERNAL ENVIRONMENT

Economic conditions in the 1980s and technological advances profoundly influenced the USPS work environment. Mail-sorting machines and laser barcodes on envelopes meant that thousands of postal jobs were to become obsolete. The pressure to compete with private delivery services like FedEx, UPS, and Purolator drove the USPS to replace paid workers with machines. Instead of mass layoffs, post offices began cutting hours and finding ways to fire employees in order to cut back the workforce. Job insecurity was extremely high in the postal service both during and after the mail-sorting and barcode-reading technology was introduced.[10]

ORGANIZATIONAL STAGE

At the time McIlvane was being mobbed, the Royal Oak postal center appeared to be in Early Bureaucratization while attempting to restructure some of its work processes to match technological changes required by the USPS. Unfortunately, these efforts were not sufficiently coordinated with needed changes in strategy, culture, and leadership.

As a result, the technological initiatives further increased the job strain of employees as they experienced less control and increased demands. Unfortunately, these conditions fostered an environment in which mobbing was highly likely.

Rethinking What Happened at Royal Oak

As in similar murder sprees preceded by mobbing of the shooters, it seems that at the Royal Oak postal center the constant pressure exerted by managers had a decidedly negative impact on most if not all workers. Based on past behavior, Thomas McIlvane was predisposed to react violently in particular situations. When he became the target of ongoing abuse by at least four of the Royal Oak managers, his murderous actions, in hindsight, seem entirely predictable.

In the wake of the Royal Oak and other postal service shootings, the federal government commissioned an extensive study of the entire postal service. The *Report of the United States Postal Service Commission on a Safe and Secure Workplace*[13] is a sober reflection of the structure, culture, and leadership of this troubled federal agency. The study reports on an extensive questionnaire completed by postal employees throughout the nation. Postal workers were found to have more negative attitudes than employees in the rest of the national workforce about work, coworkers, and management. Postal workers believed that supervisors were the primary cause of their fear for their own safety at work. They also believed that their employer did not take action to protect them from violence, and that many managers and supervisors tried to provoke employees into violence.

In addition to data gathering in this survey, the USPS has attempted to change the way managers relate to workers. Since 1996 a number of changes in the organization have been implemented.

Investigators in 2000 devoted more than 100,000 hours to investigating incidents and threats, double the time spent in 1992. As part of their training, all managers are required to take courses on spotting and handling dangerous situations. Postal officials have also established an annual opinion survey that allows employees to rate their bosses, much like college students assess professors; the responses figure in supervisors' promotions and raises. These changes appear to be working, as witnessed by a drop in reported assaults at post office facilities from 424 in 1990 to 214 in 2000.[14]

Conclusion

This chapter began by posing the question of what causes mobbing and how best we might approach answering it. Our best evidence points to the cause of mobbing as the interaction of individual dynamics, work group dynamics, and organizational dynamics. In this and other chapters, we emphasize that both work group and organizational dynamics can and do significantly influence the behavior of individuals. We realize that this explanation may be counterintuitive to the experience of many, and certainly to the media, which often seems content to attribute the causes of mobbing primarily to the individual pathology of its victims, perpetrators, or both. Focusing on the interaction effect of individual–work group–organizational dynamics in explaining the cause of mobbing is much more than an academic exercise. It has practical implications for preventing mobbing and reducing its devastating effects. Because work groups and organizations, as well as individuals, are a part of the cause of mobbing, they also have to be a part of the solution.

What It's Like to Be Mobbed

I N THE WORKPLACE, MOBBING MATTERS BECAUSE WORK matters. Work is a principal source of meaning for most people. Indeed, just having a job can be a profound source of meaning. Think about those you know who have lost a job or were unable to find a job in the last five or six years during what we now call the great recession. Not to have a job is a source of shame and fear. Shame because one isn't being productive in the way that most people understand personal productivity; fear because, for almost everyone, a job is a prerequisite for obtaining the basic necessities of life. Work is also a primary source of social contact and connection with others—a site of joint projects that we do with each other and from which we derive a sense of accomplishment.

For most people, work is a place where we do things with others in order to accomplish specific goals. Along the way, we cooperate, we have disagreements, we resolve the disagreements, we socialize, we develop goals for our work projects and strategies for accomplishing those goals, and we work alongside other people day in and day out. In fact, a person starting in the workforce at age 21 and retiring at age 65 will spend more than 90,000 hours of his or her lifetime working, most of it with other people. Given that work satisfies our needs for human connections and personal and shared accomplishment, and provides the means for maintaining an acceptable standard of living, it is no surprise that mobbing has been called a "violation of the soul."[1] Humiliating, discrediting, and ongoing attacks designed to drive one from the workplace strike at the heart of who a person is and what a person needs to do in order to survive in the world.

What is it like to be mobbed? Heinz Leymann's description of mobbing as "psychological terror"[2] still provides the best answer to that question in the fewest number of words. But how does such terror present itself in the workplace and what does it look and feel like to its victim? The description and illustration that follow are designed to provide you with an experiential sense of what happens during a mobbing from a victim's perspective and how such a victim may feel and respond. If you or someone you love has been mobbed, you are likely to recognize a number of the features and feelings associated with mobbing that are described here. This illustration highlights the social isolation that is a classic part of workplace mobbing and reactions of the target-victim to it. In the illustration, the target-victim is looking back on the events of the mobbing, providing details, and sharing reflections about it.

The Experience of Being Mobbed: Early and Mid-Phases

The mobbing started about nine months ago after you questioned your new manager's policy for workload assignment. Respected by your coworkers as a forthright and outspoken person, you spoke up not only for yourself but also for them when you challenged the new policy that effectively removed staff input into workload distribution. You felt that the new manager was reducing morale and incentives by reverting to an old-fashioned authoritarian system of workload assignment that ignored staff input. You spoke up at a staff meeting—one of the first staff meetings with the new manager—and expressed your point of view and requested that the new policy be reevaluated. Although they didn't say anything out loud, you felt supported by your coworkers and assumed that the new manager's silence was thoughtful reflection. You were wrong. The new manager saw you as uppity and as a direct threat to his authority. The first thing that the new manager did after the staff meeting was request your personnel file and schedule a meeting with the human resources (HR) director and with your supervisor. The process of digging up dirt on you had already begun. You, naively in retrospect, didn't have a clue about what was happening. Your focus was on getting the policy changed. The staff meeting was the triggering event, and over the next few months you would become more miserable at work than you had ever dreamed possible.

Nine months later you are still on the job, although it is getting harder to show up every day. Since the staff meeting both your supervisor and coworkers have actively distanced themselves from you and no longer seek your input about current projects nor assign you to new ones. You wonder how long you can tolerate the situation and what management is planning to do next. You are not sure what you are supposed to be doing work-wise or how to respond to the increasing social distancing of your colleagues. You've asked your supervisor what projects he wants you to work on, but you haven't received any clear response from him.

You sit in your office with your door almost closed. Your stomach is churning, and the sense of anxiety you feel bubbles up inside and washes all over you. You can hear some of your coworkers outside in the hallway. In the past, you would have stepped out of your office to chat with them or called out to say, "Hi." Not now. They are no longer people with whom you feel safe. You used to feel safe with them and even enjoyed being around them, but not now, not since it all started. They're talking and laughing, and they know you are in your office. There is little chance that one of them will knock on your door or poke their head around in a friendly greeting or acknowledge in any way that you are in there. You hear your supervisor outside talking to the secretary and some of your coworkers. He doesn't come by your office either.

You have become a nonperson in your workplace. You have become invisible—and you experience that invisibility both in terms of how you are treated at work and in terms of how you feel. Other people act as if they don't see you, and your whole mind and body react to that experience of being unseen and inconsequential. Your contribution to your workplace no longer seems to count or matter. Not only does it no longer count, but you can hardly make a contribution because you have been shut out of key meetings and removed from the distribution lists for emails about current and future projects. You are still a member of your workplace, but the writing is on the wall that you won't be for much longer. One way or the other, you are finished in this workplace, and you are beginning to understand that.

Capitalizing on Social Distancing in Mobbings

- Since a typical American spends more than 90,000 hours at work during his or her lifetime, social connections and friendships will inevitably develop.
- One of the early signs of mobbing is social distancing. Increasingly, the target is isolated and ostracized.
- Betrayal by coworkers who may have become friends with the victim or interpersonally significant to the victim is common in mobbing.
- The organization capitalizes on the social distancing common in mobbing by taking actions to further separate and isolate the target from coworkers. These actions are likely to include holding meetings about the target without the target, asking coworkers to document and submit to them any concerns or difficulties they may have had with the target, and posing leading questions in an investigatory phase that presupposes the target-victim to be problematic.
- Conflict that is normal and expectable in the workplace, when it involves the target, is used by the organization to depict the target as not a team-player and as out of step with an organizational culture of cooperation. Differences and conflict at work are normal, expectable, and fairly frequent and are as much a part of group life as cooperation. They are two sides of the same coin.

You play the events of the last nine months over and over in your mind, and the part that drives you crazy is that you know there are key pieces of information about the course of events that you don't have. You keep trying to piece together a coherent picture of the events leading up to and during your experience of workplace mobbing, but you are missing important information that makes it difficult to develop an accurate timeline. You realize that in the early phase of the mobbing you were unaware of what was going on—you didn't really have a clue that there was an orchestrated attack against you under way. Many mobbing victims describe this early phase of a workplace mobbing as "being in the dark," "being blind-sided," "like a deer in the headlights," "being in the twilight zone." Looking back, you realize that you only gradually became aware of what was happening at work and that you became more self-protective as your trust in your coworkers and supervisors plummeted. Nevertheless, you believe that you did the best you could to carry on at work under the circumstances and to keep up with your commitments outside of work.

You went to a family reunion in the fall, and you remember sneaking off and sitting by yourself at an outdoor café staring at the harbor and the street life around it but not really taking anything in and certainly not enjoying it. Your stomach was acting up again, and your thoughts kept returning over and over to work. You wanted to enjoy the reunion and your family and friends but you couldn't; in front of your family and friends you put on the best face you could and then retreated to your room where you could sit by yourself and try to piece together the events of the mobbing. You had this need to understand what happened to you at work and why.

Not surprisingly, you have more questions than answers. How did you become the target? Why weren't you given access to the information that your supervisor and managers had gathered about you in their investigation of the instigating set of complaints that emerged after that initial staff meeting with your new manager? More to the point, why weren't you given access to the details of those complaints? Why were your coworkers initially supportive, and, then, seemingly in lockstep, did they turn against you? What was said about you in those meetings to which you were not invited? Why did your coworkers start to pull away from you—gradually at first, but then aggressively—to the point that they ignored you in the hallway or when they saw you in the parking lot? Why were you sent a memo from your supervisor demanding an explanation for why you made 18,000 copies on the copy machine during the previous month when such usage was patently absurd and your supervisor knew it? Why were you being questioned repeatedly about two laptop computers that had turned up missing from the store-room when you knew nothing about the loss or theft and you knew that you weren't the only master key holder in your department? Why did multiple staff members in several departments know your long distance telephone code and copier code and why were they using them with such abandon? Why did your recent performance evaluation include global negative statements about you and refer to incidents that occurred long before the annual review period in question?

Why, when you returned unexpectedly one evening to your office after hours, did you find the guy from information technology (IT) kneeling in front of your computer terminal with the door to your office closed? When you complained, why did his boss not know anything about what he was doing in your office and why did your boss, who was higher up in the organization, know all about it and tell you some transparently foolish tale about upgrading your computer? And how could this IT guy even look you in the eye now anyway, when he had come to you a few months earlier asking you for a loan? And, in hindsight, you realize what a fool you had been. You liked the IT guy and had loaned him the money against your better judgment. Of all people, how could he not tell you what he was doing in your office and who had put him up to it?

The innuendos about the missing laptop computers were especially troubling because you prided yourself on being honest to a fault and you thought everyone knew that. When you first heard about the missing laptops, you just assumed that they hadn't been logged in properly or that whoever had them would bring them in after the reminder memo had been sent out to all staff members. But the computers didn't turn up, and your supervisor questioned you repeatedly about when and why you accessed the computer store-room and your procedures for logging out equipment. You under-stood that your supervisor had to use due diligence in trying to find the missing computers, but you began to feel that the finger of sus-picion was being pointed at you.

The situation with the IT guy brings to mind your relationships with other coworkers. Over the past few years you worked closely with a group of coworkers who constituted your primary workgroup or team. You regarded three or four of them as friends even though you didn't socialize with them much outside of work. You developed a sense of trust and mutual respect with these coworkers that you had come to value. You shared some of the details of your personal life with a few of them as they did with you.

In fact, one of your coworkers, who was a single parent and who had some medical problems, had asked you if you would keep a sealed copy of her will with forwarding instructions. She explained that she had changed her will recently, and she wanted to be sure that if she passed away suddenly her mother and kids would have the most recent version. You were surprised by the level of trust this coworker placed in you, but you agreed to accept the sealed will and then tucked it away. Since then you had heard that her betrayal of you to your supervisors and other managers at the height of the mobbing was egregious—that she denied trusting you or being friends with you, that she agreed you were difficult to work with, and that she passed along every piece of information about your family life that she thought she had known (much of it inaccurate). You were saddened that she never said goodbye to you when later you finally quit your job or that she never bothered to call to see how you were doing afterward—this from a person who had entrusted you with her will.

As you have done repeatedly since, you questioned your own judgment about whom you had decided to trust and realized that you had become fearful of trusting others and generally more suspicious. It never occurred to you until the events of the mobbing unfolded that sharing even a little information about your personal life at work may have been a dangerous practice and not in your best interests.

By this time your coworkers have stopped communicating with you. There was an irony to their involvement. They observed you in the process of being denigrated and cast aside by your organization, and some fully participated in that process. But when the mobbing was in full swing and the writing clearly on the wall that you were either going to be removed from the organization or effectively neutralized within it, your coworkers worked even harder to keep their distance from you. They were likely to deny their own betrayals and involvement in mobbing you and, when asked about you, responded with sanctimonious platitudes like "It's too bad, things just got to be too much for him."

You're Being Mobbed: This Is What You, Your Coworkers, and Your Supervisors Will Do

- You feel like you are in the dark about key events affecting you in your workplace.
- Information that you need to respond to and complaints about you or your job performance are heavily filtered or kept from you entirely. Typically, even if a complaint originated about your job performance, it morphs into a complaint about you and then a personal attack.
- Previously friendly and supportive coworkers begin to distance themselves from you. The social distancing is reciprocal. As the target, you have a felt sense of being isolated and ostracized, and in response as a self-protective strategy, you also distance yourself from those whom you see distancing themselves from you.
- Coworkers, one by one, betray you. To start with, these betrayals are couched in the language of concern, "Yes, he was having a really hard time with his divorce. His daughter was smoking pot and doing drugs and I know he had a hard time concentrating. It's been a tough time for him." The betrayals multiply, and sooner or later the language of concern in which they were initially couched drops away: "He's become kind of moody, and it's anyone's guess how he will respond to a request for more information about the project." And, finally, the complete betrayal, perhaps after you have filed a complaint or grievance: "He's encumbered from all of this, yes, I can see why it might be better for the team if we replaced him" or self-interest and the absence of any concern for you: "Look, I want to keep my job. I'll say whatever you need me to say." These betrayals are particularly devastating to you, because, if you have been in the job for any length of time, workplace camaraderie and friendships have developed that are now shredded, and the normal and expectable

exchanges of personal information that are a part of work life are grotesquely misused to hurt and mob you.

- Negative characterizations, gossip, innuendo, false information, and half-truths about you are distributed throughout the organization and remain unchallenged by management and your coworkers. An unflattering, and sometimes sinister, new story of you and your job performance has been constructed and circulated.
- Over time, your mistrust deepens and you experience the entire organization as unwelcoming and hostile.

Your Supervisors and the Organization Are Now Fully Involved

After you finally forced yourself to accept that there was a concerted campaign of abusive behavior directed toward you, you complained to your supervisor. You started by sending emails describing the abusive behavior and the inaccurate and unfair characterizations of you. After taking his time, your supervisor finally responded with very brief messages saying that he was sorry you were feeling distressed. With a few of these kinds of email exchanges in hand, the unsettling feeling that you were not being taken seriously began to take hold. After a few more similar email exchanges it was clear from the way your supervisor framed his responses that you were being characterized as overwrought and over reactive. He added that it was your responsibility to work out difficulties with your coworkers.

His response didn't make much sense. How could you find out who was misusing your long distance telephone and copy card codes so egregiously? How could you figure out who took the laptops from the computer storeroom? How could you usefully respond to the snickering in the hallways when you walked by and the acts of isolation and shunning that were now part of everyday work life for you? How could you make sense of the surreptitious presence of the IT guy in your office after hours when his boss didn't even know why he was in there? How could you defend against a written warning that your supervisor had sent to you without even asking for your side of the story before sending it out? You began to see the shape of things to come in your workplace—you were on your own—and the unfairness of it all was staggering.

Nonetheless, you persisted in trying to explain your perspective on the events surrounding you in your workplace, and your supervisor finally scheduled a meeting with you to discuss your concerns. He had asked an HR representative to be present. You were surprised when you saw the HR rep at the meeting because your supervisor hadn't mentioned to you beforehand that she was going to be present. You were just glad that he had scheduled a meeting so that you could talk about your concerns, and you even thought, foolishly as it turned out, that the presence of the HR representative might be helpful to you. But the meeting didn't go as you had hoped. From the outset, your supervisor put you on the defensive by asking you why you had sent so many demanding emails, and he repeated that solving problems with your coworkers was your responsibility and that you needed coaching about how to work better as part of a team. That you had become upset by your work situation was also troubling to your supervisor, who suggested a referral to the Employee Assistance Program (EAP) so that you could get help dealing with your emotions.

And then there was the question of your work record and job performance. Your supervisor had pulled out memos from several years earlier in which you were mentioned in one way or another. One memo was from a coworker who said that you did not complete your part of the work-group project in a timely way and that your work was "not up to standard." You had never seen that memo before and never knew that it existed. Not only that, but none of your coworkers or your supervisor at the time had ever addressed the situation with you before. The memo was years old, but it was brand new to you now. They also presented you with another memo from several years earlier that you had never seen before. This memo was written by a coworker whom you admittedly had never liked and who had since left the company. She had complained to your supervisor that you had been taking too much time off work and that you had not been pulling your weight and that the burden of your unfinished work had fallen on her. At first you didn't know what she was talking about in the memo, but then you remembered that when your father had had surgery several years ago you had taken some half days off over a six-week period to help your mother care for him and get him settled in rehabilitation. You didn't remember slacking off on your work responsibilities, but it was so long ago and no one had ever addressed the issues with you anyway until this meeting.

These memos were presented to you as part of the "evidence" that, in fact, it was you who were the problem and not anyone else. The memos seemingly materialized from nowhere. You had never seen them before. The issues included in them had never been discussed with you by anyone. The memos were not part of your personnel file because you had very recently requested and received a copy of it. You wondered who had been keeping those kinds of memos for so long and where they had been kept and who had access to them. You also wondered why the memos were being kept in the first place since no one had ever addressed the issues with you at the time. Fear gripped you, and you felt so weak you thought you would pass out. The writing on the wall was getting bigger, and you were feeling more alone than ever and absolutely unsure about what to do next.

The Experience of Being Mobbed: Elimination Phase

If you can stomach the ostracism and your new status as a nonperson and if the organization decides to let you stay while they marginalize you more or less permanently, you may still have a place to go that you can tell others is your workplace but that, in reality, is a place where you and your work are no longer wanted and you have been neutralized. You won't matter. Conversely, your status as an outcast may be chewing up more than your stomach, and neither your health nor your family relationships can survive the torment of workplace mobbing and you elect to leave. If you choose the resignation option, the organizational management or administration, your supervisors, and coworkers who have participated in your mobbing will be cheering you on. In fact, there will be celebrating, laughing, and high-fiving when the personnel manager phones your supervisor and division manager to let them know that you have just quit. As Hugo Meynell[3] suggests, if you quit they will have the ready-at-hand platitude to trot out about you, "The fact is that she was unhappy here, and really wanted to leave." If the organization doesn't neutralize you enough to allow you to remain, or if you don't elect the resignation option, the only other possible ending for a successful mobbing is for you to be discharged, terminated, fired. In each of these outcomes, your humiliation and elimination have been successful. You have become the most recent face of mobbing in your workplace.

Humiliation and Elimination: How Successful Mobbings Play Out

- Your professional and personal reputation is damaged and possibly destroyed as a result of innuendo, gossip, incomplete information, and uncorrected false information that has been distributed throughout the organization.
- You are left out, ignored, marginalized, and shunned by coworkers and supervisors, many of whom you formerly counted as friends or colleagues. You are not paranoid; you really are being excluded, but the organization will deny it. As the mobbing progresses you may indeed become a little paranoid and for good reason.
- The organization values its reputation as a "good and fair place to work," so it neutralizes you by demoting you, giving you work below your skill and competency level, deliberately keeping you out of key information loops, and effectively isolating you rather than firing you.
- The toll the mobbing has taken on your physical and mental health, on your sense of personal and professional identity, on your beliefs about the world as a fair and just place, and on your family relationships is too much for you. You are almost physically sick every time you enter the building. You can't or won't take it anymore no matter what the price (you'll learn more about the price you will pay as time goes on), and so you quit.

- You get terminated. They have fired you. The organization has successfully targeted you as a misfit. You are difficult, hard to get along with, unstable, a bully, you speak your mind, you resist and protest injustice to you and/or others in the workplace, you ask too many questions, you have family problems or personal problems, you are not a team player, you talk back and you talk up. Notice that "you don't do good work" or "you are incompetent" isn't in the list of personal/occupational characterizations that precede mobbing.

Personnel Files and "Shadow" Files

In the above illustration of what it's like to be mobbed, the supervisor presented unflattering memos about the target-victim that were several years old and that the victim had never seen before. These negative memos were pulled out at the height of the mobbing. They raise the important issue of "the file" and how materials in employer-maintained files can be used to harm targets in workplace mobbings.

Materials in personnel files, if damaging, have the potential to ruin a person's career and to undermine his or her ability to make a living in the future, and what's in them should be of particular concern in a mobbing. Because personnel files are maintained by authorities within an organization and access to them by the employee is generally subject to restrictions, the dynamics of power are always at play when considering such files. Organizational authorities have power and control over personnel files while employees who are the subjects of the files are in most situations permitted only to respond to negative narrative accounts about them. The dominant story is set and narrated by the employer. Unless organizations have clear and specific guidelines pertaining to the materials that are permitted to be kept in personnel and related files and governing who has access to the files, it is difficult for employees to challenge either what's in the files or who has access to them.

Supervisors, managers, and administrators in hostile organizational cultures have a penchant for keeping documents and other materials, no matter how old, that they think might be useful in the future if they want or need ammunition against an employee. We refer to these kinds of potentially damaging files as "shadow" files because they contain information about employees not included in personnel files but to which certain managers, administrators, supervisors, and clerical staff have access. Organizations that keep such files may label them as "confidential files," "private files," "supervisory files," "supervisory notes," or "supervisory logs," among other labels. The material in these "shadow" files is almost never given to employees requesting copies of their personnel files because the kind of material contained in them is not allowable in personnel files. Personnel files should only contain fact-based information about an employee.

The shadow files that are of concern to us may contain opinion and other unsubstantiated information. Examples of potentially damaging information that might be contained in the shadow files of an organization that keeps such files include random opinions about an employee from the HR department, supervisors, or other coworkers; gossip; innuendo; uninvestigated or unexplored complaints; unfounded allegations; rumors; personal opinions about an employee's work product and character; and any other type of information about an organizational member that is not factual, not the result of findings from a legitimate personnel procedure or formal process of inquiry or investigation, or not required by law. These shadow files and the information contained in them are not easily accessible to employees. Not all organizations keep such potentially damaging shadow files, but the ones that do tend to be more prone to mobbing. Storing negative material about employees in separate files is an indicator of a hostile organizational culture.

In careless organizations, this kind of shadow material may find its way into an employee's formal personnel file, opening up the organization to liability for defamation. In mobbing-prone organizations that are more careful about protecting themselves from liability, such shadow material is generally kept in separate files and may be pulled out during a mobbing to help stack the deck against a target. Some HR professionals recommend that supervisors maintain supervisory notes in a private file that is separate from the personnel file.[4,5] In mobbing-prone organizations, supervisors are much less likely to have been trained to include only factual material in their supervisory files and are more likely to include information that is unsubstantiated. So-called private files that are kept separate from personnel files are still subject to discovery in legal disputes in most jurisdictions. Additionally, recent legal precedents have expanded an employee's right to obtain copies of material in such supervisory or similar files in some jurisdictions.[6]

We take the position that it is unethical practice and abuse of power for organizations to stockpile information about employees that could be used at some point in the future to damage them. We also take the position that the burden of proof is on the organization to demonstrate the ethics of maintaining so-called private files about employees and to show cause for why it is necessary to do so.

Mobbing-Related Losses

In a mobbing, the losses pile up fast. They mount and multiply. In the early stages of a mobbing, losses begin with loss of trust in cowork-ers who have participated in negative and abusive acts toward the target-victim. The sense of loss of trust mounts as betrayals, both small and large, become known to the target-victim. It is not uncom-mon for this loss of trust in coworkers to be generalized to loss of trust in others, and the target-victim can become more suspicious of people in general. A psychiatrist[7] who has studied mobbing reminds his psychiatric colleagues that coworkers and bosses might really be out to get your patient, and it's worth checking it out before diagnos-ing him or her as paranoid.

As the social distancing and shunning that is present in mobbing progresses, the obvious loss of social connection, respect for one's contribution to the workplace, and the camaraderie and interpersonal relationships that made life at work interesting and enjoyable are the next to go by the wayside. Social connections and social relation-ships matter. Even if the relationships were only work-based, being isolated from the normal give-and-take of social life in the workplace represents a huge loss. The loss and injury is compounded when the work relationships are important to the target-victim. Feelings of shame and bewilderment go along with loss of trust and loss of workplace-based social connections.

Modern studies in neuroimaging reveal that the brain registers the experience of social rejection in the same areas that it registers physical pain.[8] These images go a long way toward explaining why the experience of rejection and the more encompassing experience of ostracism hurt so badly. Rejection, shunning, segregation, and ostracism cause both physical and psychological pain. They punish the body and lay waste to the spirit. Because we, as human beings, have a basic need to belong in order to survive and thrive, the ostracism of mobbing sends shock waves through our relationships and just about every other aspect of our lives. The social exclusion that is central to mobbing is both physically and psychologically painful.[8]

How Social Exclusion at Work Gets Justified

In order to sustain ostracism, social exclusion, and, ultimately, elimination in a mobbing, narratives to support the legitimacy of those processes have to be constructed. The best kinds of narratives to support ostracizing and excluding someone in the workplace are narratives of degradation. To create a narrative of degradation in a workplace mobbing, all the bits and pieces of negative and pejorative characterizations of the target-victim, the gossip, the innuendo, the allegations, the half-truths, and the inaccurate information must be woven together to create a story that at least has surface coherence to it. It's important that the narrative hold together or the mobbing is likely to be unsuccessful in its goal of eliminating the target-victim from the workplace.

Like lots of stories, narratives of degradation can last and follow individuals around, sometimes for the rest of their lives, ruining their opportunities for meaningful re-employment and, in some cases, for any employment at all. In the process, of course, the target-victim's reputation is compromised and damaged, often beyond repair. The moral of the story of these narratives of degradation and their attendant power is that these stories are dangerous, and when we hear them we ought to regard them as suspect. The losses that come from such harmful narratives are huge—no job, compromised re-employability, damaged reputation, and the shattered sense of personal and professional identity that follows such injuries.

Work matters to people, and it matters a lot. In the United States, without a job a person will almost certainly lack affordable health insurance coverage. A target-victim successfully eliminated from the workplace due to mobbing also will lose opportunities to continue to contribute to company pension or retirement plans. The mobbing victim now minus a job is hurt in the pocketbook through loss of income, loss of health benefits, and loss of opportunity to participate in company retirement plans. These financial losses are both present and future.

In the immediate aftermath of being fired or quitting as a result of having been successfully mobbed, a target-victim is unlikely to have a grasp of the full range of losses that are associated with being mobbed. In a sense, a mobbing never ends because the effects of having been mobbed and the associated losses endure. Loss of trust in others, loss of social connections, rejection and ostracism, loss of a job, and damage to one's reputation affecting both one's sense of personal and professional identity and re-employability all have significant negative impacts on physical and psychological health. This negative impact on health is thoroughly documented in the literature and is substantial.[9] In addition, mobbing affects the quality of family relationships because the target-victim isn't the only one who lives through the mobbing—the whole family does—and each member of the family is hurt in different ways as a result.

Mobbing-Related Losses

- Your reputation has been dragged through the mud and the negative stories circulating about you have hurt you more than you care to acknowledge.
- You've been isolated in the workplace and ostracized. You ache with both emotional and physical pain as a result—and that is not hyperbole, it is science.
- You cared about your work and your contribution to your company. The quality of your work product mattered to you. Your work gave you a sense of meaning and dignity. The attacks on your work and

on you as a person were searing and struck at your identity—both personal and professional.

- You've lost your work and social relationships with your coworkers. You recognize how much those relationships meant to you and you grieve over some of them.
- You lost your job, your health benefits, and your opportunity to continue participating in your company's retirement plan. You've been hit hard financially, both in the short term and for the future. Your financial security is not what it was before you lost your job.
- The future is frightening and you are insecure about how you will provide for yourself and for your family. You live with a sense of dread and foreboding.
- Your confidence in yourself and in your ability to rebound has been seriously damaged. The personal and professional assaults in mobbing have come at you from so many sides that regrouping is much more difficult than you thought it would be, especially if you're older.
- Your health has suffered. You are depressed and anxious. When you get a cold or flu it takes you longer to recover than it used to, and since the mobbing began you've had bouts of chest pain and gastrointestinal problems.
- It's bad enough that you had to experience the devastating effects of being mobbed, but that your family was forced to go though it with you and suffer the ripple effects themselves added injury upon injury.

Conclusion

Most people who go to work, at whatever level in an organization, are excited to have a job, excited to have the opportunity to work and contribute—especially in this post–great recession era. It is quite stunning then to realize, over time, that one has become the target in a mobbing. Mobbing involves experiences that most people would work hard to avoid—being denigrated, humiliated, abused, and eliminated from one's workplace. Mobbing leaves workers who are generally competent and caring about the quality of their contributions to their workplaces feeling as if they have been cut from their moorings—at sea, bereft, and uncertain about what their futures will hold.

The point of providing an experiential illustration of what it's like to be mobbed, as we have done in this chapter, is twofold. First, those who have been mobbed can recognize elements of the experience and feel less isolated and more understood as a result. Second, those who have no personal experience with mobbing can begin to appreciate its destructive and encompassing character. With between one-third and one-half of American workers experiencing negative acts directed toward them on a weekly basis,[10,11] understanding experientially what it's like to be mobbed will hopefully draw more people into the conversation about how to prevent mobbing and improve psychological safety in the workplace.

How Mobbing Affects Health and Well-Being

M OBBING MAKES PEOPLE SICK. IT AFFECTS THEIR physical, psychological, and emotional health. It also brings with it an array of psychosocial effects that impact a person's beliefs about people and the world. The same person who found it easy to trust and rely on others before being mobbed in the workplace becomes suspicious, mistrustful, and always on guard afterward. Likewise, this same person who saw the world as generally fair and just before being mobbed becomes cynical and sees the world as unfair and threatening after being mobbed. Over time, people build up mental frameworks or schemas for how they see the world and make sense of it. These frameworks help people to understand themselves and give meaning to their lives. That these frameworks for making sense of life are frequently shattered in the aftermath of mobbing has enormous implications for how mobbing victims can reclaim and recover meaningful lives afterward.

Mobbing also strikes at the heart of a person's occupational or professional identity, corrupting the experience of work and disrupting its continuity. Damage to one's reputation, job disengagement, and problems with reemployability are another set of effects with which people who have been mobbed must contend. Taken as a whole, the physical and psychological health consequences of mobbing, the impact on social relationships and core beliefs that people

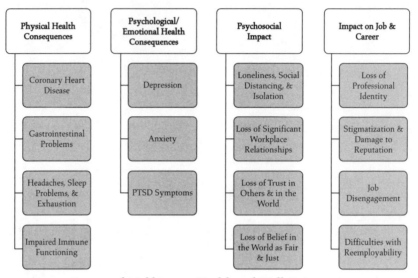

FIGURE 5.1 Impact of Mobbing on Health and Well-Being.

hold about themselves and the world, and the unanticipated job and career challenges create a daunting set of new circumstances for mobbing victims. Every mobbing victim will experience some form of injury to her or his overall health and well-being and job outlook and prospects. The degree of injury will be determined by the severity of the mobbing, the cumulative history of previous trauma,[1] the victim's capacity for resilience,[2,3] and the quality of the social support system surrounding the victim.[3] Figure 5.1 summarizes these effects of workplace mobbing on health and well-being.

Negative Health Consequences Are Injuries, Not Illnesses

Teasing out the difference between an injury and an illness is not as straightforward as it may seem, but the difference is critical to understanding what happens when people are mobbed at work and then begin to experience physical and/or psychological health problems. An injury is a harm sustained by someone or a harm inflicted on someone, and the term is used to designate physical injuries suffered as a result of accidents from a wide variety of causes, ranging from swimming mishaps to car crashes to wars. The term *injury* is also used to designate harms and losses inflicted unfairly, irresponsibly, or negligently on someone by others. *Illness*, conversely, is the term used to designate a disease or disorder of the mind or body or the subjective experience of such a disease or disorder.

In our previous book on workplace mobbing we described its negative physical and psychological health effects at length.[4] These health effects range from an increase in the experience and intensity of headaches to the onset of heart disease to major depression to post–traumatic stress disorder (PTSD), all the way to sudden death and suicide. Study after study has demonstrated that being a victim of workplace mobbing is associated with a likelihood of increased health problems.[5–15] Consequently, it is more accurate to identify these negative health consequences associated with mobbing as injuries rather than as illnesses.[16,17]

In some cases, the negative health consequence will be something the person has never experienced before. In other cases, the negative health consequences will be an aggravation of an existing health problem. An injury (or illness) is considered to be work-related by the Occupational Safety and Health Administration (OSHA) of the United States "if an event or exposure in the work environment either caused or contributed to the resulting condition or significantly aggravated a pre-existing condition."[18] The association between the health problems discussed in this chapter and the strength of the research supporting an association between them and workplace mobbing is more than robust enough to satisfy OSHA's requirement that the workplace event or exposure either caused or contributed to the negative heath consequence or aggravated a preexisting health problem.

Physical Health Injuries from Mobbing

It makes sense that most people who think about the negative health effects of workplace mobbing and other forms of interpersonal abuse in the workplace will think first about the effects on a victim's psychological and emotional health. Workplace mobbing, although on occasion including acts of physical aggression and violence, consists primarily of acts of non-physical interpersonal hostility and abuse. Interpersonal abuse is associated with the most severe negative health consequences of all forms of trauma, especially in terms of psychological health.[19] Nonetheless, being victimized through workplace mobbing is also associated with an array of physical health problems that can either be new or exacerbations of existing conditions. It would be a mistake for mobbing victims, their health care providers, and family members to overlook the significant and troubling physical effects of mobbing because the psychological and emotional effects often are so overwhelming.

So what are the most documented physical health effects of mobbing? The answers may be surprising. Coronary heart disease, either through the onset of new disease or the exacerbation of existing disease, is associated with workplace mobbing.[6,7] Gastrointestinal problems are also associated with the experience of workplace mobbing, as are headaches,[15] sleep problems,[12] and generalized fatigue and exhaustion.[12] Those who have been mobbed at work have also shown evidence of impaired immune functioning, which, by definition, will make victims more vulnerable to other health problems.[6,12]

In identifying health consequences of mobbing, both physical and psychological/emotional, you will notice that we use the term *associated with* rather than *caused*. There is a reason for that. Most research about medical and health effects of a particular stressor concludes that a stressor (for example, workplace mobbing) can be clearly associated with a range of health effects or problems. To say that a particular stressor actually "causes" a particular set of health problems involves a standard of proof that is frequently not available in the medical and behavioral sciences. It took decades for medical scientists to be able to state unequivocally that tobacco "caused" lung cancer even though repeated, robust associations between smoking and lung cancer were present long before scientists were actually able to make that causal statement. Research about mobbing and health consequences has increased considerably since the 1980s but is not yet at a point where causal relationships can be identified. What can be identified though are strong associations between the experience of workplace mobbing and the negative health effects that we describe. Whether the injuries experienced by a target-victim of workplace mobbing are psychological or physical in nature or both, they are better understood as *what happened* to the person and not as what is wrong with the person. Understanding individual responses as arising from what happened to a person who has been mobbed rather than as what is wrong with that person is consistent with the distinction between an injury and an illness.

Workplace Mobbing and Post–Traumatic Stress Disorder (PTSD)

One of the most frequently cited anxiety disorders associated with workplace abuse is post–traumatic stress disorder or, more commonly, PTSD. Heinz Leymann, the psychologist who conceptualized and named workplace mobbing, also developed a clinic to help its victims. Leymann believed that the most common and accurate diagnosis for persons who had suffered negative consequences from workplace mobbing was post–traumatic stress and related disorders.[8,20]

The traumatic event that sets off the series of intense symptoms associated with PTSD is the ongoing workplace abuse to which the victim has been subjected and from which the victim finds it difficult or impossible to leave or escape. We take the position of a number of researchers[21,22,23] who have found ample evidence that a variety of traumatic events, not just acute life-threatening ones, result in symptoms of PTSD. Keep in mind that in the current flagging economic climate, which has been the norm for a number of years now, it is not easy for a worker to think about quitting or leaving a job. The financial stability and well-being of that worker and worker's family depends on the income, health, and retirement benefits from his or her job. Leaving a job in today's economically fragile environment is no small matter.

When a worker is caught up in an abusive work context, leaving is attractive because it means the prospect of escaping workplace abuse. At the same time, leaving is also frightening because it means uncertainty about obtaining future work and providing for oneself and one's family. Workplace mobbing victims are commonly caught up in these kinds of double binds in which all of the known options are unattractive. The idea of being "caught up," "captured," "entrapped," "powerless" in a situation in which victims feel helpless or powerless has led to the description of certain forms of PTSD as *complex PTSD*.[24] The experience of PTSD as a result of workplace mobbing can be viewed as complex post–traumatic stress disorder (C-PTSD) because of the interpersonal abuse that is central to it, the chronic or ongoing nature of workplace mobbing, and the sense of entrapment that comes from feeling that most or all options to resolve it are bad options. It might be surprising to learn that nonsexual workplace abuses like mobbing are associated with worse outcomes than sexual harassment.[25]

Tim Field, the prominent antibullying advocate in the United Kingdom who worked tirelessly until his death to provide support for those who, like him, had been bullied, set up the richly resourced "Bully OnLine."[26] Field also believed that PTSD was a common outcome for those who had been bullied in the workplace, and he was one of the first to describe how post–traumatic stress symptoms manifest for victims of workplace bullying. In this section on PTSD and in the section on depression that follows we have followed Field's lead and described the kinds of symptoms of post–traumatic stress that mobbing victims are most likely to experience in the same way that Field did for victims of bullying.

To do so we have used common negative behaviors in workplace mobbing and target-victim reactions to them[5,8,13,14,16,20] so that victims and their families will be able more easily to identify and make sense of symptoms they are experiencing or witnessing. It is important to keep in mind that an individual target-victim may experience none, some, most, or all of these symptoms and that individual reactions to traumatic experiences like workplace mobbing can vary widely. Remember that a mobbing victim's cumulative personal history of trauma,[1] capacity for resilience,[2,3] and level of social support[3] will influence the degree to which he or she experiences symptoms. Recognizing these or similar PTSD-like symptoms in oneself or in a family member who has been a target-victim of workplace mobbing suggests that the target-victim is responding to the abusive events with traumatic symptoms and should obtain psychotherapeutic help.

What Happened to the Target-Victim of Workplace Mobbing

- A person (target) has become the victim of workplace mobbing in which there has been a concerted, ongoing effort to remove him/her from the organization through a campaign of questioning and raising doubts about the victim's workplace decision making and the quality of his or her work products; removing the victim from key meetings and other information loops while at the same time denying that the victim has been left out of the information cycle; talking about the victim behind his/her back and suggesting that other organizational members document in detail any concerns or problems they may have had with the victim; fabricating or exaggerating information about the victim's personal and family life and mental stability and spreading the inaccurate or false information in the workplace through gossip; clear and noticeable social distancing and isolating from the victim on the part of other coworkers and key managerial and administrative personnel.

Mobbing-Related Traumatic Re-Experiencing Signs and Symptoms

- When the target-victim realizes what is going on and understands that he/she is the victim of a series of ongoing hostile and abusive interpersonal acts in the workplace, the victim responds both with disbelief and with a sense of helplessness and terror about both the immediate and longer-term future.
- The victim ruminates on the traumatic workplace events and thinks about them over and over down to the most minute details of what happened; who did what and when; dwells repeatedly on why he/she became the target-victim, comes up with no good answer, and starts the cycle of ruminating on the mobbing all over again. Images of the key instigators and key players involved in the mobbing enter unwelcomed into the target-victim's mind, and the victim is disgusted, disturbed, and saddened by them.
- Nightmares become a regular feature of the victim's nightlife, and images and snippets of aspects of the mobbing appear in dreams, often in terrifying forms.

- When the victim thinks about the mobbing or tells stories about it to others it is as if it is happening in the present. The affect and emotion surrounding the events are raw and exquisitely painful.
- The victim can't drive by the workplace or see the name of the workplace or other signs and symbols of it without experiencing feelings of distress. If the victim is still working where the mobbing happened or is happening, walking into the building each day is difficult and disturbing.
- Being reminded of the mobbing or having to go to work in the place where it happened is accompanied by feelings of dread and anxiety. The victim experiences physical symptoms like tightness in the chest and stomach, clenched fists, sweaty palms, and tachycardia, together with a sense of helplessness and loss of control.

Mobbing-Related Traumatic Avoidance Signs and Symptoms

- The victim of workplace mobbing actively tries to avoid thinking and talking about the traumatic experiences associated with the mobbing. The act of trying to push the mobbing experience away only serves to connect the victim more to it. Trying not to think about and remember the details of the mobbing just brings them more to mind.
- While many, if not most, of the coworkers with whom the victim worked have already distanced themselves, the victim's previously cordial and friendly relationships with coworkers no longer exist, and the victim feels used and betrayed. As a result, the victim has lost trust in his/her coworkers and reciprocally distances from them even more. The victim actively

avoids coming into contact with signs and symbols of the workplace and can't even drive by the place of work where the mobbing occurred without feeling sick and full of anxiety.

- As is consistent with those who experience many different kinds of trauma, the mobbing victim has a hard time recalling details and specifics of the traumatic events.[27] It is easier for the victim to say in a general way, "I was treated very badly at work," than it is for the victim to recall specific, detailed events.

- The end result of workplace mobbing is ostracism and social exclusion. The body reacts to social exclusion and ostracism in the same way it reacts to pain—it hurts and, often, very badly.[28] When the victim is dealing with both emotional and physical pain and is ruminating over the events of the mobbing, previously important interests, activities, and other pursuits are left aside.

- Workplace mobbing is a violation and destruction of formerly important human relationships in the workplace. The victim invariably loses trust in others and, as a result, distances and isolates from them. Because of the preoccupation and pain associated with mobbing, the victim may also transfer that sense of mistrust and distance to other social relationships, including those with family and friends.

- Emotional numbness is associated with social exclusion[29] in general and with workplace mobbing in particular. It is not only common but should be almost expectable for a mobbing victim to feel emotionally numb and drained, especially during the early and peak phases of a mobbing.

- As a result of the trauma of workplace mobbing, the victim often gives up on the idea of having a meaningful career or any career at all. Given the impact of mobbing on one's job and career trajectory, the person mobbed may well have very good reasons for feeling gloomy and pessimistic about a future career, believing that his/her best days are over. This sense of pessimism and foreboding is easily extended to include relationships and family, given that a career is central to most people's ideas about what is essential to have in order to sustain a relationship and family life.

Mobbing-Related Signs and Symptoms of Increased Arousal

- The experience of being mobbed puts a victim in the surreal context of having to come to terms with a set of workplace events that is difficult if not impossible to make sense of. The result of the normal and understandable need to make sense of such situations is that the victim spends a lot of time thinking about the events, replaying them, and wondering if and how he/she could have done anything different to stop or reverse the mobbing. The end result is a chronic state of being keyed up and agitated. Sleep does not come easily for a mobbing victim, and the anxiety associated with the whole experience makes falling asleep especially difficult.
- Being keyed up, irritable, and quick to anger are common responses for those who have been mobbed. Some victims remain emotionally numb and don't understand why they do not have strong feelings of anger toward the perpetrators. Other victims become outraged at the injustice, humiliation, and betrayal that they experienced and remain in a protracted state of anger. For others, anger and outrage build slowly over months and years as the victim puts pieces of information together and realizes more about who the key players in the mobbing actually were and what they actually did.

- Memory is impacted by the trauma of workplace mobbing as it is in other forms of trauma. In addition, the parts of the brain that are responsible for forward planning, concentrating, and problem solving are not as readily accessible[27] for many mobbing victims as they are for those who have not experienced trauma.
- Having been traumatized, hurt, and betrayed during a workplace mobbing by coworkers and their hostile behaviors, victims are in a state of heightened alert in an effort, often unconscious, to recognize other incoming threats.
- The outcome of living in a state of keyed-up agitation and of constantly scanning the environment for incoming threats is an exaggerated startle response to anything that is unexpected.

For mobbing victims, identifying and understanding their emotional and psychological reactions is often the start of healing. Anxiety symptoms, like those associated with PTSD, are not the only psychological problems linked to mobbing. People who have been mobbed also often end up sad and depressed both about what has happened to them and about what they think their future holds.

Workplace Mobbing and Depression

All lives have ups and downs, and work life, in particular, can be expected to have its share of both. However, the experience of being mobbed is one of the "down" times from which it can be difficult to recover. Depression is a common psychological condition that is frequently associated with mobbing.[6,11,12]

At one level, being mobbed and pushed out of a job might seem like a negative life event that people could get over without too much difficulty. Some people can and do. But not all do. For most people, work is central to their survival—it's how they make a living for themselves and those they care about and how they pay their way in the world. Work is also about belonging to something larger than oneself, and the relationships that are part of the workplace support that sense of belonging. When work is recognized as central to survival and belonging, it's a lot less surprising that many victims don't easily get over workplace mobbing and go on to develop symptoms of PTSD and/or depression. Here we describe how the symptoms of depression are likely to manifest for victims of mobbing.

Mobbing-Related Signs and Symptoms of Depression

- People whom the victim trusted and counted on as coworkers have spread false information about him or her or stood idly by and done nothing while others spread the misinformation, exaggerations, and lies. The victim's feelings run the gamut from disbelief to denial and from sadness to anger.
- The victim is angry at his or her coworkers some of the time but often doesn't feel much of anything because of an overwhelming sense of emotional numbness. At other times the victim directs the anger inward toward him- or herself for thinking it would all blow over and for not fully grasping the seriousness of the situation.
- Being criticized repeatedly at work, excluded from access to information and resources needed to do a good job, lied about, and isolated from and by coworkers and supervisors is excruciatingly painful. The victim is in emotional and physical pain.
- The victim keeps thinking and hoping that someone at work will finally stand up for him or her and let coworkers and supervisors know that he or she has been a loyal and conscientious employee and that what has happened is neither fair nor right. But no one stands up or comes to the rescue, and the injuries of betrayal and social exclusion are magnified for the victim.
- Feeling fatigued and exhausted, the victim has little or no energy for work, family, or fun. Previous interests

and activities are no longer appealing. The victim has trouble concentrating and thinking through the events of the mobbing and making decisions about what to do about his or her work situation. The victim is confused and uncertain about whom to talk to and trust. Coworkers are out of the question, and the victim notices that family members are running low on patience themselves, so soliciting their help doesn't seem like a good idea either. The victim feels overwhelmed and lonely. The victim alternates between obsessing about what happened at work and trying too hard to put it out of his or her mind. Finding a comfortable middle ground seems almost impossible.

- The victim blames him- or herself for not recognizing earlier that he or she was the target of a concerted series of hostile workplace behaviors and feels guilty for denying and minimizing what was happening and just hoping it would all go away.
- The future, especially the work future, looks gloomy and hopeless. The victim feels blindsided by what happened during the mobbing and can't easily visualize a better work future. Self-recrimination and feelings of worthlessness commingle with the hopelessness.

What depression looks like for a mobbing victim can be easily tracked in Laurel's story that follows. Laurel was a physician in a busy women's health care center. A brief discussion with a nurse following a procedure in which Laurel felt the nurse had been both unhelpful to her and inappropriate to the patient rapidly escalated into a mobbing situation.

A Physician's Story

Laurel was a radiologist in a large urban comprehensive health care center where she specialized in women's health and, in particular, in breast health. She was a highly regarded diagnostic radiologist and had specific expertise in digital mammography and MRI for detecting breast tumors and other women's health problems. In addition to her radiology practice, Laurel was also an active clinical faculty member in the school of medicine at the state university in her area. Because of her role in women's health, Laurel had frequent interactions with patients and the whole patient care team. About seven months ago, she critiqued a nurse over a patient care issue and was stunned to find herself as the subject of a formal complaint to the hospital administration by the nurse the very next day.

While preparing a patient for a needle biopsy, the nurse became exasperated with Laurel's repeated requests to adjust the patient's positioning due to the patient's large breast size. The nurse then made what she thought was a humorous comment to the patient about her large breasts, and the patient became upset. After the procedure, Laurel spoke to the nurse and reminded her about the importance of maintaining a professional demeanor during all procedures, especially when they are challenging. For Laurel, that was the end of it. For the nurse it was just the beginning.

Laurel went through what she described as a humiliating investigation of the complaint that Laurel felt was essentially an attack on her personally. The nurse who had filed the complaint and other nurses on the same patient care team had, in Laurel's words, "publicly attacked her as being a poor communicator, not a team player, and indifferent to the concerns of both patients and nurses." The complaint was dismissed as unfounded, but Laurel's troubles had hardly begun by the time the investigation of the initial complaint was over. Since then the nurse who had filed the complaint and her coworkers had made a point of giving Laurel the silent treatment whenever they saw her, spread malicious gossip around the hospital both about her professional competence and her personal life, routinely "misplaced" patient files and reports that Laurel needed to do her work, and adopted a "work-to-rule" or "do only the minimum necessary" approach toward assisting Laurel in her duties as a physician.

Laurel thought that the dismissal of the nurse's complaint had only served to accelerate the series of hostile behaviors directed toward her by the nurse and her group of coworkers. She had been to the human resources department at least three times in the past seven or so months and was told every time that there was nothing they could do because the behaviors were not indicative of hostile behaviors targeted against her as a member of a protected class. Laurel said that she wished the group would make comments about her religion or national origin or something else so that her HR department would do something.

Because of the nurses' ongoing hostility toward her, Laurel felt that she had to be constantly on the lookout to protect herself and her patients and found herself second-guessing her decisions at work and doubting her own competence. Laurel acknowledged that she had become paranoid but stated that her own career and the safety of her patients required it. Over a seven-month period, Laurel went from being a highly regarded physician who looked forward to going to work every day to one who dreaded even the thought of going to work. She said that her job had turned from one she loved into one that was making her sick and that she felt both helpless and ashamed for feeling so helpless.

Laurel was isolated at work and because of family and other considerations couldn't realistically look for a job elsewhere. She had little energy or enthusiasm for work, for her kids, or for her responsibilities as a mother and looked forward to getting into bed every night as early as she could. Laurel was seriously depressed, and she knew it. She also knew she had to get some help to deal with her depression and the workplace abuse that had triggered it. She was stuck, she said, and the whole ordeal was taking a toll on her, her marriage, and her family life.

Psychosocial Impact of Mobbing and Resulting Losses

Being victimized by workplace mobbing inevitably results in damage to one's personal and professional reputations. An ongoing series of hostile acts directed toward a target at a workplace is going to be noticed, sooner or later, by coworkers, supervisors, and subordinates. Since one of the hallmarks of mobbing is exclusion from the group and ultimately the workplace or, minimally, a particular unit of the workplace, others will eventually notice the victim's isolation and social distance from everyone else. Even if such workplace onlookers had nothing to do with the hostile acts that were a part of the mobbing and knew little or nothing about them, they will still wonder why the victim is isolated and seems standoffish. Invariably, the onlookers will attribute the victim's behavior to personality characteristics rather than to the operation of group and organizational dynamics. The difference in behavior will be attributed by others to something about the victim rather than to something about the workplace.

Damage to the victim's reputation is, in the end, the result of a series of public or private acts that enter into the free flow of information about a person. Disparaging comments about a worker's personal and professional life by participants in a mobbing are designed to hurt the target. Coworkers may wonder whether the negative news circulating about a worker is true or not. By that point, the damage is already done because the participants in the mobbing have successfully introduced confusion and uncertainty about a worker's personal and occupational or professional identities.

The message that gets telegraphed amid the confusion and gossip about the victim is that the victim is no longer a person who can be thought of and trusted in the positive way in which he or she was previously regarded. Once negative information about a worker enters a complex system like a workplace, it cannot be called back. Like trying to put toothpaste back in a tube, it can't be done. Workers who have been mobbed labor under the influence of a stigma that is very difficult to cast off.

For a worker like Laurel who prized her high standards of patient care, having her commitment to her patients called into question during a mobbing undermines both her personal and professional identities. A caring person is central to how Laurel has seen herself since before medical school and through graduating and starting her medical practice. Caring, competence, and commitment were the three values that organized Laurel's sense of herself. Much as she tried to hold on to her core understandings of who she was, the workplace abuse she had experienced took its toll, and Laurel found herself second-guessing her behavior and mistrusting those around her in the workplace. These are not small effects; in fact, they are huge. How Laurel saw both herself and others in the world was undermined, and rebuilding a view of both herself and others that she could rely on would turn out to be a laborious process.

Modern work settings involve substantial emotional labor. The emphasis on teamwork, relationship-building, communications processes, collaboration, and collaborative decision making requires the development of interpersonal skills and emotional intelligence. As a result, most workers come to place a high value on their relationships at work. So much so that the sociologist Arlie Russell Hochschild[30] suggests that especially for dual-career, time-scarce parents or caregivers with children, home becomes work and work becomes the place where overburdened parents can find some peace and solace. Then factor in being targeted as part of a mobbing, and not only one's identity but also one's highly valued work relationships and sense of home away from home are suddenly gone.

Laurel is a good example of someone who, before she was mobbed, believed that the world was basically a fair and just place. After being mobbed, she no longer saw the world that way. She shakes her head and wonders how the group of nurses could have been so vicious to her in the first place and how they were able to get away with it with such impunity. Laurel saw her private complaint to one of the nurses as justified because she felt that the quality of patient care was at stake. She wasn't out to hurt the nurse but rather to improve patient care. Laurel, like many mobbing victims, could not understand how her intentions and actions had become so maligned and misinterpreted. In hindsight, she actually didn't know if she would have done anything differently had she to do it over again. Laurel believed she still would have made the complaint to the nurse about the patient care issue because she saw her job as protecting the welfare of her patients.

Effects of Mobbing on Career Path

For mobbing victims, career damage spirals outward, reproducing itself into the future. If you've been mobbed and you got fired or quit, try getting a decent job reference from your previous employer. It's very difficult because, as the person mobbed, you have already been constructed as the bad apple in your work group or organization. You have been forced into a situation where you have to "manage" the fact of your termination or quitting. Mobbing is hugely disruptive of careers. It throws a wrench into a victim's career path and pushes that person onto a path not of their choosing. Because of the difficulties involved in getting positive job references after being mobbed, some mobbing victims believe that they will not be able to get another job in their field within an organizational setting. Others have become uneasy and are afraid to go back to work in an organization.

As a result, it is not uncommon for mobbing victims to begin to work for themselves or to become entrepreneurs. Mobbing represents a significant discontinuity in a person's work life, and the prospect of beginning to work independently or becoming an entrepreneur is often a choice that the mobbing victim feels pushed to do in order to be able to continue working. Working for oneself or becoming an entrepreneur, while it may work out very well, often was not the mobbing victim's first choice.[31] It is a solution to the problem of having a career derailed after being mobbed.

For those who have been mobbed and who are still in their jobs and organizations, work withdrawal and job disengagement are common responses.[32,33] It cannot be surprising that a worker who has been humiliated and abused in various ways and who remains on the job might show up in person but not in spirit. Such workers generally carry out their work functions as best they can under the circumstances but don't do anything extra and participate with coworkers as little as possible, primarily as a way of protecting themselves from further hurt and harm. Their sense of commitment to the organization and to their job will most likely have diminished. Mobbed workers still on the job are also likely to be absent more frequently than normal, to use up their sick leave, and to exhaust their medical leaves of absence.

For better or for worse, our jobs and careers become a central part of both our personal and occupational or professional identities. We have been hearing the question, "What are you going to be when you grow up?" from as early as first or second grade, and we make small talk and edge around getting to know someone in social settings by asking, "What do you do?" or "Where do you work?" When someone has been pushed out of a job as a result of mobbing, it's the mobbing victim who has the most trouble with those questions and what they mean. In part, we understand ourselves and our place in the world through our work history. When mobbing disrupts that work history, our understanding of who we are in the world shifts, sometimes dramatically.

In our experience, it is the norm more than the exception for mobbing victims to doubt themselves and their worth and to question their competence and ability to function in the give and take of the workplace. Some mobbing victims find a way back to work within an organizational context, while others do not. One thing, however, is certain, and that is that the meaning of work for a person who has been mobbed is forever changed and decisions about future work flow out of that experience. If mobbing victims go back to organizational life it is with a sense of vigilance, even hypervigilance, and reduced trust both in their new coworkers and in their new organization. Mobbing victims who go back to organizational life monitor themselves more closely than before and monitor others in the workplace more closely also. As noted, some don't return to organizational life and decide to work independently, no matter what that means in terms of reduced income and benefits or the demands of starting up a new business venture.[31]

For those who decide not to return to organizational life after being mobbed, going back is too frightening and risky or it is not a realistic option because of the damage done to their reputations and the difficulty in obtaining a positive job reference. Some mobbing victims don't return to work at all because of the negative impact on their physical or psychological health and well-being. Whether mobbing victims return to work or not, how they view work and the workplace is altered forever. Months and even years after being mobbed at work, victims talk about living their recovery every day.

Conclusion

The health and mental health injuries that mobbing victims sustain tend to be chronic and long term rather than acute and short term. As a result, these injuries have an erosive quality on mobbing victims' lives, infiltrating their social relationships, their beliefs about the world, and just about everything else. Mobbing victims, even after they are fired or quit, are left lonely and mistrustful of others. While they want new social relationships they are afraid of being harmed all over again and are understandably reserved and often suspicious. At the least, mobbing stalls or temporarily derails careers. At the worst, mobbing destroys careers, and its victims are faced with career decisions they never dreamed they would have to make—decisions like whether to change career paths entirely or go into business for themselves—not because they want to but because they feel they have no other choice. Whether the career impact from mobbing is temporary or permanent, mobbing victims are forced to deal with the damage to their reputations and the stigma left behind by workplace abuse and humiliation. The greatest damage of all occurs when victims internalize the "we don't want you here" message of mobbing and respond by believing that they are worthless.

Mobbing Has Multiple Victims

W ORKPLACE MOBBING HAS A WAY OF INCLUDING others, apart from the victim, in the grip of its damaging effects. Mobbing takes a toll on intimate relationships and interferes with the exercise of parenting responsibilities, thereby affecting children. Workplace mobbing affects partners, spouses, and children, and some suffer secondary victimization. The impact on family members can be significant as can the impact on workplace bystanders who witnessed all or part of a workplace mobbing and abuse event. Workplace bystanders tend to respond similarly to the primary victim in terms of negative health and career effects, but not quite as intensely. Organizations, the incubators of workplace mobbing, do not escape the negative effects of mobbing and are subject to a range of both direct and indirect costs as a result. It is not enough to just understand the destructive impact of mobbing on the direct victim because that is only part of the story. Those who love the victim, those who depend on the victim, those who have worked alongside the victim, and the organization itself all pay a high price for workplace mobbing. We describe that high price in this chapter.

Impact of Mobbing on Family Life

Family life, parenting, and sustaining loving, intimate relationships involve a lifetime's worth of work and commitment. The rewards can be big but so can the challenges. Stress is a normal and expectable part of both couples' relationships and parenting. But not all stressors are the same. Kenneth Westhues has called mobbing "the stressor to beat all stressors."[1] While that might sound dramatic, when you consider the insidiousness of mobbing and the way it eats at just about every major aspect of a victim's life and how losses pile up in its wake, mobbing as "the stressor to beat all stressors" begins to make sense. In this section, we will look at the impact of mobbing on both intimate relationships and on parenting. Let's start with couples' relationships.

Couples' Relationships

Most people enter into committed relationships with another person because they want closeness with that person and because they want to build and share their lives together. Closeness and intimacy just don't happen, of course, and these highly prized qualities of a relationship require attention and care to achieve. Like the proverbial third wheel in a relationship, mobbing gets in the way of intimacy. To understand how, let's look first at the evidence from the professional literature[2] that tells us what the key features of closeness and intimacy in couples' relationships actually are. Then we'll look at how mobbing does damage in couples' relationships. The following list[2] describes behaviors of partners in a couple's relationship that are central to the development of intimacy and closeness.

- Commitment to the relationship
- Awareness and mindfulness of the relationship
- Trust and authenticity
- Mutuality, mutual understanding, and mutual support
- Mutual responsiveness and warmth
- Sharing confidences and mutual self-disclosure
- Actively working to decrease relationship tension and conflict and to improve relationship quality by developing relationship repair skills

- Increasing positive perceptions of the relationship
- Sexuality and sexual relating
- Creating shared meanings

Taken together, these relationship qualities and skills are at the heart of closeness and intimacy for couples. They describe the characteristics of good communication, attention to the relationship, expression of affection and warmth, and the development of shared understandings and meanings that just about every article on how to have a good relationship endorses and that partners in couples' relationships desire. Succeeding at closeness and intimacy in a relationship takes directed actions and attention on an everyday basis. When workplace mobbing enters the picture and a partner in a couple's relationship becomes the victim of mobbing, the entire landscape of the relationship is changed. Mobbing is what happens to the victim, but it also happens vicariously to the victim's partner. Consider this example.

Matt and Phil were a same-sex couple living in a midsize college town in the South. Matt worked as an engineer at a global construction company with a small regional office in his town. Phil was back at school working on an advanced degree in nursing and hoped to become a nurse practitioner in oncology. Matt and Phil had been in a committed relationship for seven years, and they had agreed that Phil would quit his nursing job in order to go back to school full time. Matt had transferred within his company to the regional office in the town where Phil had received a partial scholarship from the university. Because they would be living in a smaller town and expenses would be lower, Matt and Phil were not worried about living on just Matt's salary while Phil went back to school.

While the town was not gay-friendly in the way that large metropolitan cities were, it was not gay-unfriendly either. There was an identifiable gay community and enough awareness about gay, lesbian, bisexual, and transgender (GLBT) issues that many stores and small businesses posted rainbow pride "safe place" and "all families welcome" stickers in their windows. The trouble was not with the town but with Matt's workplace. Two divisional managers ran the regional office where Matt worked. Matt was accustomed to the macho culture of the construction company where he worked, but he had never experienced it as hostile until he transferred to his current location.

The managers were both heterosexual married men, with teenage kids, who had been reasonably successful in their careers with the company. It took Matt a while to understand what was going on in their office, but at some point he got the whole picture.

The two managers had taken to going out with a variety of young women at lunchtime, having extended lunches with wine and cocktails, and coming back to work several hours later. These extended lunches had been going on for several months, and the managers would goad Matt by inviting him to pick up his girlfriend and join them when they clearly knew that Matt was gay and in a committed relationship with Phil. When they weren't out of the office, the sexual and homophobic innuendos from the managers became a staple of office banter between them. Matt privately believed that the managers were both homophobic and sexist. As much as Matt disliked the homophobic innuendos that peppered the office talk he found the demeaning sexual references to women just as offensive. Things got worse when the two managers decided to hire as receptionists three of the women with whom they were having these lunchtime affairs. Only one had any office skills to speak of, and the managers enlisted the three as office tattletales. The managers told the new receptionists that they wanted them to keep a special eye out for Matt because he had a hard time fitting in and wasn't a team player.

Matt wasn't one of the good old boys, and he was paying the price for that. The two managers sent Matt on regular overnight and weeklong trips to meet with clients and suppliers under the ruse of helping him to learn "every facet of the business, especially on the supply side." Matt was usually gone on one of these trips when important planning meetings were held by videoconference with the main office. Matt knew it wasn't a coincidence. Between the homophobic comments, the bogus trips to meet with small clients and suppliers, and his being shut out from the important business of the company, Matt was feeling both disgusted and afraid for his job. Matt expressed his concern to the two managers about missing the regular videoconferences and planning meetings with the head office. They responded, barely disguising the implicit threat in their words, by telling Matt that he needed to continue visiting with suppliers and the clients in the southern region so that "he would understand how things are done out of this regional office."

While Phil was enjoying his graduate studies and trying to talk to Matt about them, Matt was suffering in silence about what was going on at work. His stomach was acting up constantly, and he was turning down more and more social invitations for the weekends. Most weekends, he wouldn't even go out to dinner or a movie. Matt preferred to just stay in bed. When Phil finally asked him what was going on, Matt became angry and accused Phil of being too demanding and inconsiderate of his need to rest during the weekend. Matt yelled at Phil and told him that he wasn't interested in talking about nursing or oncology and just wanted to be left alone. Phil had never seen Matt so prickly and irritable. He also had never seen him so unwilling to talk about whatever it was that was going on, and Phil was pretty sure that the problem was at work.

Phil felt hurt by Matt and left out and alone. He and Matt had always been able to fall back on their respect and support for one another and on their willingness to talk about problems when things got stressed in their relationship. This time was different, and Phil didn't know what to do. Phil didn't know how to get Matt to start talking to him about what he was sure was trouble at work. With the silence and distance just growing between them, Phil started to worry about whether he was going to be able to finish his nursing studies. He feared that Matt was going to get fired and that Matt was just too embarrassed to talk about it. Phil's imaginings were starting to get the better of him, and he wondered what Matt had done at work that could have caused him to behave so differently than usual.

Finally, Matt told Phil what was going on, and Phil couldn't believe that the managers were able to behave so badly and get away with it. Phil thought Matt was still holding out on him, and he was sure that Matt had done something to get himself in such trouble at work—although he couldn't imagine what. The whole story was so bizarre that Phil had a hard time accepting it. He wasn't very sympathetic to Matt and privately blamed him. The distance between them had grown, and both wondered if it could ever be bridged. The irony was that Matt was being excluded and mobbed at work, and Phil was feeling left out and isolated at home.

How Mobbing Affected Matt and Phil's Relationship

- Matt's uncertainty and his efforts to understand his mind-boggling work situation resulted in his withdrawal from Phil and refusal, in the early and mid-phases of the mobbing, to talk about what was happening. Phil's desire to talk and Matt's resistance to talking resulted in a classic pursuer/withdrawer relationship that gets in the way of communication and emotional closeness. Matt was expending so much emotional energy trying to cope with his impossible work situation during the week that he compensated during the weekend by using isolation and withdrawal to conserve energy and feel better. While Matt's efforts to rest can be understood as attempts to solve a problem at one level (work-related exhaustion), they caused different problems at another level (lack of attention to his relationship).

- Matt was isolated, uncertain, and lonely at work. Phil was isolated, uncertain, and lonely at home. Matt wondered if he was going to be able to keep his job. Phil wondered if they were going to be able to keep their relationship. Matt was kept out of key information loops at work. Phil was kept out of key information loops at home. Matt was worried about whether he was going to be able to keep his job and what his future would hold. Phil was worried about whether he was going to be able to stay in graduate school and what his future would hold. This kind of parallel process is known as *isomorphism*. What happens in one domain of life is mirrored in another.

- Matt was angry and outraged about what was happening to him personally at work and about what he witnessed more generally in his toxic and unethical workplace—homophobia, sexism, and flagrant abuse of power. Lacking a framework for understanding mobbing and for describing it, Matt expressed his frustration and anger inside the relative safety of his personal relationship by venting at Phil.

- Mobbing stressed Matt and Phil's relationship to the breaking point. Matt's preoccupation with what was happening at work and his resulting exhaustion left him with few resources to attend to his relationship with Phil. For a while, Matt closed down emotionally, leaving Phil in the dark about what was going on and without the necessary information to be helpful. The lack of attention to their relationship, the lack of communication, the emotional distancing, and the lack of

Common Emotional Reactions by a Partner or Spouse to Workplace Mobbing

- Bewilderment
- Uncertainty and confusion
- Blaming
- Irritability and anger
- Fear about the future
- Fear about the relationship
- Social and emotional distancing
- Worry and anxiety
- Sadness

understanding of each other's needs during the mobbing left both Matt and Phil feeling isolated, unsupported, and emotionally distant. It wasn't just Matt who was suffering from being mobbed. Phil was also suffering.

Partners and spouses experience a whole range of emotional reactions to the workplace mobbing of their significant other. These reactions parallel the emotional experiences of the partner who has been mobbed, leaving both parties in the relationship hurt and in need of support. When both are hurting, it's much harder for each to know what to do to help and support the other. Displaced anger, venting, and criticizing are common responses, even understandable ones given the context of having to endure workplace mobbing as either the primary or secondary victim, but they are not helpful responses. The following chart offers samples of the kind of talk likely to inflame and make matters worse between partners as well as samples of the kind of talk likely to help and soothe. The helpful and unhelpful talk presented here is based on our own clinical experience and is informed by extensive research[3,4] concluding that successful couples are emotionally attuned to one another, handle conflict and negative emotions in gentle, soothing ways, and have developed effective relationship repair skills.

Talking to Your Partner or Spouse about Mobbing

What Doesn't Help (Either You or Your Partner/ Spouse)	What Helps (Both of You)
That's unbelievable. I've never heard of anything like that before. You must have done something wrong.	That must be so difficult for you. Can you share more of what's happening at work and tell me more details?
How do you expect me to help you if you won't talk about it?	This is too big for any one person to deal with alone. I don't want you to have to carry this burden all by yourself.
I'm not the one who treated you so badly at work. Why are you taking it out on me?	Can we talk about the hurt and outrage that you feel?
It's been months and, if anything, you seem worse than you were before. Can you just let it go and let's move on?	I know you need time to get your head around everything that's happened and to recover. I'm right here with you.
What are we going to do? This doesn't just affect you, you know. We're all affected, and I don't know how we're going to make it if you lose your job.	This is a really tough situation that we are in. I think it would be a good idea if we sat down and tried to look at all of our options carefully and then begin to make some decisions.
I can't take this anymore myself. It just goes on and on and gets worse and worse. I don't know how I'm going to handle this whole situation.	I think we need a breather—some time out so we can get a better perspective. It's probably not a good time to make decisions about our relationship or work and money right now. Maybe we should consider getting some professional help.

Parenting

For those with children, being a good parent is an almost universal goal. While nearly every parent wants to be caring and effective, the greater challenge lies in knowing what to do in terms of concrete actions to turn that desire into reality. The basics of good parenting include presence, both physical and emotional (not constant but consistent), and attention. When a parent has been mobbed in the workplace, the effects don't just trickle down to the children, they pour down. We can examine the effects of mobbing on parenting by looking first at what the evidence has to say about the basic ingredients of good parenting and then looking at how mobbing interferes with that mix. The good parenting behaviors that we will look at are the big skills—the overarching attitudes and behaviors that effective parents use most of the time and that have evidence[5,6,7] to back them up. Then we'll look at how mobbing gets in the way. The following list[5,6,7] includes parenting behaviors and skills strongly associated with good outcomes for children.

- Presence, attention, caretaking, supervision
- Maintaining an emotional connection with your child
- Fostering competence and skill-building
- Modeling desirable values and behaviors

Parenting takes physical and emotional presence. Obviously that doesn't mean that a parent has to be with the kids all of the time. What it does mean is that parents need to be present both physically and emotionally to their children on a consistent basis. Emotional presence involves being aware of how a child is feeling and knowing how to respond empathically to a child within the context of being a parent rather than the child's best buddy. To be emotionally present and responsive to a child requires focus and attention and enough room in the parent's head to keep track of how the child is doing and what special needs the child might have at any given time. Attention to the needs of a child of any age also includes age-appropriate caretaking and effective supervision.

The workplace mobbing of a parent affects children in the family in immediate and potentially long-lasting ways. A parent who is in the throes of a workplace mobbing or who recently either has been fired or has quit because of mobbing is a preoccupied parent. The mobbed parent is going to be preoccupied with the humiliation and losses experienced, often to the point of obsessively ruminating over details of what happened, mentally replaying the events over and over, and spending large stores of energy trying to make sense of a social process of elimination that is very difficult to make sense of much less to accept. Preoccupation with the key players and events in the chronology of the mobbing is a typical response to workplace mobbing and doesn't begin to encompass the acute preoccupation, withdrawal, and impaired focus and concentration that occur in more severe mobbing injuries like depression and PTSD.

A parent preoccupied by workplace mobbing will be less able to provide the attention and the emotional and even the physical presence needed to parent consistently and well. Because so much of a parent's focus and concentration is subsumed by the events of the workplace mobbing, parental caretaking and supervision will also be negatively impacted. Since workplace mobbing, by definition, lasts months and even years,[8,9] a parent who has been mobbed can reasonably be expected to have a reduced attention span and increased preoccupation with the mobbing for lengthy periods of time, affecting not just the victim's well-being but the well-being of any children.

Maintaining an emotional connection to one's children is a key feature of good parenting; this connection is especially important as kids get older and move into adolescence. Children and teens who feel loved and cared about do a lot better than kids who don't have that sense of emotional security in their lives. The kids who feel loved and secure are less likely to engage in high-risk and dangerous behaviors. When things get tough between parents and their kids, the emotional connection between them is a lifeline that parents can use to bring their kids' behavior back within an acceptable range. While maintaining an emotional connection to one's children is a labor of love, it is still a labor and that labor requires energy, focus, attention, and concentration—the resources in shortest supply when a parent is dealing with the effects of workplace mobbing.

Kids who learn how to do things in the world and who learn how to do those things well do better than kids who are showered with praise without having the praise linked to actual efforts and results. Parents who help children and teens build real-world skills, from the most basic to the complex, are helping their children lay a foundation for lifelong success. Skill building is competence building, and competence leads to confidence. A small child who puts out the dog's food every evening and who plants and waters vegetables with his mom and watches them grow is developing skills and learning how things work in the world. So is an older child who is learning to play the guitar and taking Spanish lessons. Such efforts genuinely deserve the compliment "good job." Parents play a significant role in creating the context within which kids learn how to do things and to develop skills. In early childhood, it's skill-building parents who take the time to help a small child learn how to get out the dog's dish and pour the dog food rather than doing it themselves because it's faster and makes less of a mess. Later on, it's still the parents who support the sports activities, language classes, music lessons, and the hundreds of other activities that kids want to try out for size.

Helping children and teens build skills from talking to reading to rowing takes a tremendous amount of time and effort. Much parental involvement in helping children learn how to do things goes unnoticed because it becomes part of the weave of everyday life. But reduce or take away a parent's participation in the process of helping their children to build skills and that drop in parental involvement will become apparent in no time. Workplace mobbing robs a parent of the energy and motivation needed to keep pace with the daily demands that are part and parcel of helping children to build skills and learn how to do new things. The longer the parent has been robbed of the energy and motivation required to stay engaged with a child's skill- and competence-building requirements the harder it is on the child. Parents who are exhausted, preoccupied, and depressed from being mobbed at work are much less likely to be responsive to the assortment of demands placed on them by their children than are parents who have not been mobbed, all other things being equal. In ways both small and large the mobbed parent's availability and responsiveness to a child is significantly diminished. If workplace mobbing happens to a parent during a critical time in the child's life or development and the parent is exhausted, preoccupied, irritable, or emotionally unavailable, the impact of the mobbing on the child will potentially be magnified.[10,11]

Parents who model socially desirable values and behaviors help their children to do likewise. From helping out around the house, to being respectful and kind to others, to doing homework regularly, children learn from what their parents do. For example, parents who keep up with the housework, who treat others with respect, and who follow through on their own work commitments are teaching daily lessons to their children that are more powerful than verbal exhortations to do those things. For parents who have been mobbed at work, it is very unlikely that they will see either the world or their workplaces as they had before. Mobbing victims have their views of justice and fairness turned upside down. They are less likely to regard their own personal world, including their workplace, as fair and just, and they are less likely to see the world in general as a just place either.[12] Their sense of faith and trust in the world as generally fair has taken a beating.

For parents who have been mobbed, this splintering of beliefs in the world as fair and just gets played out in front of the kids. What may then get modeled for children is lack of faith and trust in work and, to an extent, lack of faith and trust in other people. For children and young people who need to learn how to form relationships and to trust both institutions and other people, the modeling of splintered beliefs and mistrust is especially bitter fruit. Children whose parents have been mobbed at work, like partners and spouses, are also affected by workplace abuse and suffer secondary victimization. They too will benefit from help and support.

How to Help a Parent Who Has Been Mobbed

- Keep in touch with the parent who has been mobbed. Call to say hello and let the parent know that you want to remain in contact—that remaining in contact is important to you. Don't stay away. Show up and express concern. Don't inadvertently reinforce the belief that other people are not to be trusted by not calling or stopping by. The mobbed parent is already feeling excluded and isolated.
- Keep the parent informed of family activities in the community that might be of interest or fun. Suggest that your families attend a community activity together.

- Offer to take the kids to after-school or weekend activities. This gives the parent who has been mobbed the opportunity to rest or to take care of some work-related business in private.
- Offer to take the kids out on the weekend or to stop by and help with homework.
- Invite the family over to your house for lunch or a barbecue and to watch a movie or play games. The purpose of this and the other suggestions listed here is to help the mobbed parent and his or her family feel wanted and connected to other people and to their community and, in the process, to mitigate the experience of social exclusion and shame at having been fired, demoted, or forced to quit a job.

Mobbing victims are pulled from their moorings at their work-places and ostracized and eliminated from their work communities. They experience physical and psychological health injuries, loss of job, loss of income, loss of health and retirement benefits, loss of important work relationships, and damage to their personal and occupational reputations and sense of who they are in the world. Mobbing victims also frequently come to see the world as unjust, unfair, and unsafe for them. The impact of mobbing also extends to the victim's family—to partners or spouses and to children, as we have described above. Mobbing interferes with the exercise of behaviors and skills needed to sustain intimacy in a couple's relationship and the practice of core parenting behaviors needed to effectively nurture children.

Mobbing strains family relationships and introduces multiple potential stressors into family life. Like the mobbing victim, family members also experience isolation and fear. Family members, especially partners and spouses, are often at a loss as to what to do to help. The mobbing victim has experienced direct victimization and the family secondary victimization. When everyone in the family has been injured and impacted by mobbing in one way or another, reaching out to each other is especially difficult. Everyone in the family is in need of help and support for the injuries suffered from the same event, and everyone is drawing from the same pool to try and provide that support. Strain is the inevitable result.

Bystanders Are Victims, Too

Bystanders to workplace mobbing are coworkers and colleagues who are witnesses to the systematic harassment, humiliation, and elimination of a victim from the workplace or from a unit within the workplace. Some bystanders witness the entire workplace mobbing from start to finish. Other bystanders only witness parts of the mobbing. All bystanders are affected by workplace mobbing in one way or another. By definition, a bystander to workplace mobbing is a witness to a part or all of the workplace abuse of another. The number of bystanders to workplace mobbing and abuse is high, ranging from 9% to 70% of workers studied.[13,14] The numbers of bystanders to mobbing and abuse at the high end of the range were those in higher education and health care settings.

A number of dilemmas are involved in thinking about bystanders to workplace mobbing. While the term *bystander* is used in the literature about workplace mobbing and abuse, it is often poorly defined. Bystanders to workplace mobbing cannot be thought of in the same way as random bystanders to aggressive or violent acts on the street where the bystander has no prior relationship to the victim. In workplace mobbing, bystanders have a preexisting relationship of some type with the victim. Bystanders observe aggressive and abusive acts directed toward the victim, are given firsthand accounts by the victim of the abusive acts, and/or are shown documents that confirm abusive behavior directed toward the victim. While it may seem self-evident, it is important to recognize that bystanders to workplace mobbing are independent moral decision-making agents faced with making moral decisions when witnessing the workplace abuse of another. The following are key points about the role of bystanders in workplace mobbing and the ethical decisions with which they are faced.

1. Bystanders are adult occupational and professional workers within organizations and have the capacity to make moral

    decisions about how to respond to their witnessing the abuse of another worker.

2. The basic moral decision that bystanders to workplace mobbing and harassment must make is whether to ignore what they observe and do nothing, or to do something. Doing something means either helping and supporting the victim or hurting the victim further by joining in the mobbing.

3. For bystanders in workplace mobbings the decision to do nothing is still a decision and can be thought of as an act of omission while a decision to do something can be thought of as an act of commission. Whether a bystander chooses to do nothing or to do something, the choice has moral and values implications for all of the parties involved.

4. When witnessing workplace mobbing, to paraphrase Paul Watzlawick's axiom that "one cannot not communicate,"[15] one cannot not act. Ignoring, walking away, pretending not to notice or know, standing up for the victim, or siding with the aggressors in the mobbing are all choices. All are acts with moral significance.

When considering that bystanders to workplace mobbing have relationships with one another and to the mobbing victim, the meaning of who and what a bystander is begins to get fuzzy and change. Bystanders are not apart from the workplace and victim but are very much a part of the whole network of work relationships. Their decision making about what kind of actions they will take when confronted with workplace mobbing involves them as participants, not necessarily as aggressors—possibly so, but certainly as participants. And as participants, often unwilling participants, bystanders are affected by the workplace mobbing of their coworkers in ways that mirror the injuries of the victim but at a lesser level of intensity.[16,17]

    For mobbing victims, the huge disappointment is that the choice a bystander is most likely to make is the choice to not get involved and do nothing. From the perspective of the mobbing victim that choice represents betrayal. The mobbing victim is likely to think that coworkers will come to his or her aid and defense. That they usually do not is devastating to the victim, who valued his or her relationships with coworkers and who no longer feels able to trust them. From the perspective of the bystanders, trying to keep their distance is about fear and self-preservation. Bystanders do not want to have happen to them what happened to their mobbed coworker. The fear and avoidance of the social exclusion at the heart of workplace mobbing is deeply ingrained if not primal.

Bystanders have three basic choices about how to respond to the workplace mobbing of their coworker, namely: (1) turn their back on the situation and do nothing, (2) join in the mobbing either actively or passively, or (3) support the victim either actively or passively. Each choice represents an ethical decision with a different set of implications. Bystanders most commonly turn their backs on the situation and do nothing. However, doing nothing can be interpreted in a variety of different ways by others, including the victim, and is likely to be experienced over time in a number of different ways by the bystander him- or herself. Initially, a bystander may see doing nothing as remaining neutral and as a way of keeping out of the situation. As the mobbing progresses and the victim becomes more isolated and disparaged, the same bystander may reinterpret the victim as culpable in some way and revise the meaning of his or her inaction as appropriate, changing the meaning of doing nothing from a neutral act to a consenting act.

Joining the mobbing preserves membership in the group when all signs point to the eventual elimination of the victim from the workplace. Standing up and standing apart from the workplace mob is high risk and takes courage. Bystanders can join a mobbing in both active and passive ways.[18,19] Active joining of a mobbing involves aligning with those who are already actively mobbing a victim and engaging in negative acts like divulging confidences and tainted opinions of the victim to management or administration. Passive joining of a mobbing involves remaining silent or doing nothing and allowing such inaction to be interpreted, without correction, as support for the elimination of the victim from the workplace.

Active support for a mobbing victim includes going to the victim's defense, challenging the accusations against the victim, and standing up for the victim. Passive support for a mobbing victim involves quiet gestures toward the victim indicative of concern and support and not participating in gossip or mischaracterization of the victim.

Even though they consider leaving their own jobs in much higher numbers than do employees who are neither witnesses nor victims of mobbing, bystanders typically don't want to leave their jobs as a result of being pushed out due to workplace mobbing and abuse. If they leave they want it to be on their terms, and so they either turn their backs on their mobbed coworker, or, if they offer support at all, it is passive support offered from a safe distance. It is a very small number of bystanders who don't turn away from their mobbed co-workers and who actively support them.[20,21,22]

The overwhelming majority of bystanders to workplace mobbing and abuse are distressed by witnessing it. Bystanders experience the same type of physical and mental health symptoms that victims experience, just not quite as severely.[23] Some studies have even shown that bystanders to workplace abuse suffer distress at levels higher than those experienced by first responders and emergency workers.[24] Like victims of workplace mobbing, bystanders experience a range of symptoms of emotional and psychological distress, and their overall physical health is also negatively impacted. When physiological indicators of stress are measured, bystanders have had levels of arousal and anxiety suggestive of post–traumatic stress similar to victims of workplace mobbing and abuse.[24] In addition to these physical and mental health symptoms, about 22% of bystanders[22] report leaving their jobs as a result of the negative workplace culture associated with workplace abuse and harassment.

Bystanders to mobbing are destabilized by virtue of witnessing the workplace abuse of a coworker. They are subject to a range of negative physical and mental health effects that mirror those of the mobbing victim. In addition, they are more likely to leave their jobs because of witnessing the abuse of another and because of what such abuse says about the culture of their workplace. By virtue of a role not of their choosing and that may have been thrust upon them, bystanders are drawn into the process of having to make ethical decisions about how they will respond to mobbing. Bystanders to workplace mobbing are faced with living with the implications of their choices about how to respond and what those choices mean to them, their coworkers, the target-victim, and the organization itself.

Mobbing Costs Organizations, Too

The ripple effects from workplace mobbing flow outward to encompass the victim, partners and spouses, children, other family members, friends, and bystanders to the mobbing within the workplace. The categories of people negatively affected by workplace mobbing are sizeable, and the damaging effects are costly at many levels. But the damage and hurt are not limited to individuals and families. The organizations themselves that are the incubators of workplace mobbing also pay a heavy price.

Workplace mobbing and other forms of workplace abuse expose organizations both directly and indirectly to higher costs. Mobbing- and abuse-prone organizations incur direct costs through higher turnover and lower retention. Turnover represents direct costs in terms of job searches and retraining. There are also indirect costs associated with high turnover related to the hard-to-quantify loss of highly skilled and talented employees. Other indirect costs relate to low job morale and job dissatisfaction as a result of work- place mobbing and abuse. Employees who are dissatisfied with a mobbing-prone workplace culture are less likely to be engaged and productive than satisfied employees working in high-care workplace environments.

Direct costs from workplace mobbing and abuse include those associated with medical leaves of absence, sick leaves, higher rates of absenteeism, worker compensation claims, and the cost of inter- nal grievance procedures and external litigation. Indirect costs from medical leaves of absence and sick leaves may show up in higher costs to the organization for employee health insurance and worker com- pensation insurance. Hard costs to organizations in the United States as a result of workplace abuse, while difficult to calculate definitively, have been estimated from between $180 million[25] to $250 billion annually.[26] In the United Kingdom, hard costs to organizations from workplace abuse have been calculated at £2 billion annually in addi- tion to an annual loss of 19 million work days.[27]

Without significant negative publicity about an abusive and mobbing-prone organization, damage to an organization's reputation will probably not be a major cost consideration for the organization. Unless forced to acknowledge mobbing and workplace abuse in the courts or in the newspapers, organizations that are mobbing-prone tend to be insular and self-protective, denying organizational prob- lems and blaming individual "disgruntled employees." The fact that there may be a long procession of such "disgruntled employ- ees" extending back in time does not seem to be much of a concern for mobbing-prone organizations. But when workplace abuse and a mobbing-prone culture do hit the news the results can be organizationally devastating and inordinately costly.

While most organizations will deny an internal problem with workplace mobbing and abuse, the large number of workers who report being mobbed, bullied, or otherwise abused in the American workplace tells a different story. Organizations pay a price for workplace mobbing and abuse, although it is a price they do not care to admit. Nevertheless, organizations are hurt too by workplace mobbing and abuse. While hard numbers are difficult to come by, it makes common sense that paying for prevention of workplace mobbing and abuse is a smarter move than paying for damages from it.

Conclusion

The effects of workplace mobbing can be devastating for the individual victim who typically suffers multiple losses, including physical and mental health problems, damage to career, and erosion of personal and occupational identities. These effects from mobbing are sufficient in themselves to think of mobbing as a totalizing experience impacting the major domains of a person's life. But this description of the impact of mobbing is incomplete. To fully appreciate the impact of workplace mobbing requires acknowledging the effects of mobbing on family and friend relationships, on bystanders who witnessed the mobbing at work, and on the organization where it happened.

Mobbing can overwhelm family members and introduce a significant amount of stress, irritability, hopelessness, and social distancing into these primary relationships. The reciprocal expectations that come with being a partner and a parent are often compromised as a result of mobbing, and both family members and the victim may have fewer available resources with which to carry out the work of intimate relationships and parenting. In such cases, everyone in the family loses.

In the same way, bystanders who have witnessed mobbing are less satisfied with their jobs and workplaces, leave their jobs more frequently, and suffer similar health consequences as the victim. Witnessing mobbing is not an easy experience and compels bystanders to make moral decisions about how they are going to respond to the mobbing and to the victim—decisions that they may not have been prepared to make. Finally, organizations also pay a steep price for mobbing that they would not have to pay if they were more willing to acknowledge the problem and get out in front of it.

Recovering from Mobbing

MOBBING PRESENTS A NUMBER OF CHALLENGES FOR both those who study it and for those who have been victimized by it and who are trying to heal. Because mobbing is so ugly a reality and its dynamics often so camouflaged under the rubrics of organizational statements about honorable missions and principled values, there has been an understandable temptation to focus on individual bullies and bullying without addressing the organizational behavior that supports mobbing. Mobbing researchers and theorists, in the relatively short time since Heinz Leymann began his work in the 1980s, have focused much of their attention on developing an understanding of what mobbing is that will hold up under scrutiny. This has been and continues to be important work.

But Leymann also spent a great deal of time trying to understand what the effects of being mobbed were on its victims and what kinds of treatments would be of most help. Those who have been mobbed get understandably impatient with the academic discussions surrounding mobbing and bullying. They might be suffering from post–traumatic stress disorder, they might have been mobbed out of a job, or they might be struggling to put one foot in front of the other and enter the building where they have suffered so much humiliation and abuse. In any case, they want help, and they want it without undue delay. In this chapter, we offer ten principles for recovering from mobbing and discuss each in detail. These principles represent practice-based evidence from our own work and are further grounded in developments and research in the areas of trauma-informed mental health care,[1] the effects of social exclusion and ostracism,[2,3,4,5] and narrative therapy approaches to surviving trauma and reclaiming personal agency.[6,7] Our intent is that these principles and their related discussions will provide a guide for the understanding and action required to heal from mobbing. Figure 7.1 provides an overview of these key strategies for recovering from mobbing.

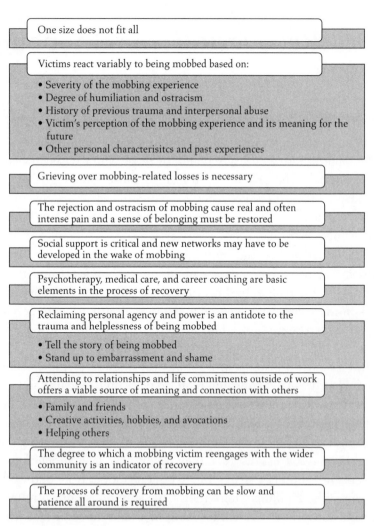

One size does not fit all

Victims react variably to being mobbed based on:
• Severity of the mobbing experience
• Degree of humiliation and ostracism
• History of previous trauma and interpersonal abuse
• Victim's perception of the mobbing experience and its meaning for the future
• Other personal characterisitcs and past experiences

Grieving over mobbing-related losses is necessary

The rejection and ostracism of mobbing cause real and often intense pain and a sense of belonging must be restored

Social support is critical and new networks may have to be developed in the wake of mobbing

Psychotherapy, medical care, and career coaching are basic elements in the process of recovery

Reclaiming personal agency and power is an antidote to the trauma and helplessness of being mobbed
• Tell the story of being mobbed
• Stand up to embarrassment and shame

Attending to relationships and life commitments outside of work offers a viable source of meaning and connection with others
• Family and friends
• Creative activities, hobbies, and avocations
• Helping others

The degree to which a mobbing victim reengages with the wider community is an indicator of recovery

The process of recovery from mobbing can be slow and patience all around is required

FIGURE 7.1 Ten Mobbing Recovery Principles.

There Is No One-Size-Fits-All Treatment for Mobbing Recovery

Heinz Leymann[8] pointed out that individual mobbings are alike in their basic ingredients; there are only so many ways an organization can mob and get rid of someone. One of the reasons Leymann made that point is so readers wouldn't think they or their friends were the subject of the case studies about which he wrote. While the elements of a mobbing and its outcome are fairly predictable, how a mobbing victim will respond is not as easily predictable and is dependent on a number of factors. Mobbing victims will respond variably depending on these factors:

- The severity of the mobbing experience
  Mobbings go on for periods of time ranging from months to years. Generally, the longer the mobbing lasts the more destructive it will be for the victim. The nature of the abusive acts and how hurtful they are to the individual victim will also influence how a victim responds. The more hurtful and damaging the victim perceives the hostile acts to be, the more injurious the mobbing for the victim. What this means is that looking at a mobbing from the outside in will not necessarily explain or predict a victim's response to the set of hostile acts. Different mobbing victims can respond differently to the same or similar abusive acts that have the same outcome of termination or quitting. The meaning that the victim ascribes to the negative acts directed against him or her and to the losses associated with the mobbing will significantly influence the response.
- Degree of humiliation and ostracism
  The more people who are involved in the mobbing, the more isolated and unsupported the victim is likely to feel. The more public the mobbing becomes the deeper the sense of humiliation for the victim. Condemnations of the victim that make their way into the newspapers, on to blogs, and into the grapevines of workplace and professional organizations deepen the ostracism and harm to the victim. The humiliation and ostracism of mobbings are intended to separate the victim from his or her community of workplace

peers. The more successful the mobbing is in making the victim feel totally isolated, the more traumatic the experience is likely to be.

- History of previous trauma and interpersonal abuse
  Mobbing is a form of workplace interpersonal abuse that is layered upon the cumulative history of abuse and trauma that a particular victim has already experienced in life. Victims of workplace mobbing who also have histories of previous traumas and other forms of interpersonal abuse are at greater risk for experiencing more protracted and more debilitating symptoms. Workplace mobbing for those with a history of previous interpersonal trauma can be a disabling blow. Trauma is cumulative; the more trauma a person has experienced in life, the more likely it is that the person will experience multiple chronic physical and psychological health problems.[9,10] Trauma victims don't get used to trauma; they become more sensitized and more vulnerable as the number of exposures to trauma mounts over time.

- Victims' perceptions of the mobbing experience and its meaning for the future
  The meaning that the victim assigns to the events of the workplace mobbing and what it portends for the future are also going to influence a particular victim's response. The more encompassing the victim perceives the effects of the mobbing to be on his or her life and future, the more profound and traumatic the injury. The more options a victim sees for life post-mobbing, the more contained and limited the damage. The fewer options a victim sees, the greater the damage.

- Other personal characteristics and past experiences
  Personal traits and levels of social support will also influence an individual's response to mobbing. How a person copes and adapts to problems in life will influence coping and responding to mobbing. Mobbing victims who have survived and thrived through difficult previous life experiences are more likely to feel that they are able to navigate the challenges of their current difficult situation. Those with social support are going to do much better than those without social support. A "keep on trucking" attitude in the face of adversity

combined with positive social support helps mobbing victims to be more resilient when faced with their losses.

While the structure of mobbing is fairly consistent across organizations in which it happens, the response to being mobbed varies considerably from victim to victim, depending on the factors we just discussed. What all mobbing victims have in common though is the need to acknowledge and grieve the losses they have suffered as a result of mobbing in order to assist in their own process of recovery.

The Need to Grieve

Mobbing in the workplace results in multiple and predictable losses for a victim. While it may be difficult to do, especially early on in the recovery process, it is important to face up to and name the losses[11] that one has incurred as a result of mobbing. Naming a loss is part of the process of developing a detailed and coherent narrative about the traumatic experience of having been mobbed. The fuller and more complete a post–traumatic narrative is in terms of the details of the mobbing and its effects on the victim and the victim's family and friends, the more likely the victim is to recover well from the trauma.[11,12] Being able to tell the story of what happened during the mobbing and to map its effects helps victims to place the mobbing experience into a context and to attribute personal meaning to it. For most mobbing victims, the experience of having been mobbed is a life-altering one that shatters previously held beliefs about fairness, justice, loyalty, personal competence and confidence, and what the future will hold.

Even though it may be quite difficult, facing up to and naming the losses one has sustained as a result of mobbing creates the beginning of a coherent narrative of loss that will ultimately allow a mobbing victim to move forward in life. Losses that remain unnamed and for which no personal meaning has been assigned are not incorporated into the evolving story of one's life and therefore cannot help the person to "restory" a sense of personal and professional identity. Unnamed losses from a mobbing hang on as disorganized yet powerful features of an individual's personal and career history and future life trajectory.

Multiple Potential Losses for Workplace Mobbing Victims

- Loss of a job and/or stable career trajectory
- Loss of income and the independence of having an income stream
- Loss of health benefits
- Loss of retirement plan and benefits
- Altered personal and occupational identity
- Damaged professional reputation
- Compromised prospects for reemployability
- Loss of personal confidence
- Shattered beliefs in the world as a fair and just place
- Loss of workplace friendships and support network
- Weakened health status and onset or aggravation of health problems
- Stress and strain on family relationships

Loss and grief are always paired. The response to loss is grief. Grief is the experience of sadness for what once was and no longer is and includes an array of other emotions like anger and fear. Grieving is the necessary response to the losses from workplace mobbing. It's just not possible to go from having a job to being mobbed and forced out of that job to bouncing back and coping well with the trauma of being mobbed without going through some transition process. That transition process is grieving. For most people, work and relationships are the two organizing features of life, and mobbing subverts both. Work is interrupted or derailed. The betrayals that are an inevitable part of mobbing result in loss of relationships that once were meaningful and fear of placing trust in others again. Because mobbing undermines both work and relationships it represents a huge discontinuity in a person's life course. That discontinuity can be bridged through active grieving.

Understanding the Pain of Social Exclusion and Ostracism

Mobbing victims would be the first to confirm that the pain of ostracism and the pain of being betrayed by formerly friendly coworkers is one of the worst parts of the experience of being mobbed. We are biologically and evolutionarily designed to be part of a group.[4] We are built for belonging because belonging is probably the best way to survive threats. Mobbing and belonging are opposites. The very act of scapegoating and ganging up on a target removes the target from the shelter of the group and sets the target up as a vulnerable outsider. Fascinating research[5] in neuroscience is demonstrating that social exclusion actually hurts in much the same way that physical pain hurts and frequently initiates a set of defensive-aggressive responses in the ostracized person. This research describes how the brain and body use virtually the same processing and regulation system for dealing with both physical and social pain.

There is a reason for this shared underlying system and the reason is that pain is an alarm alerting us to threats to our safety and well-being. Physical pain alerts us to something in our bodies that needs attention so that we can stop hurting and get well again. Social pain relating to exclusion and ostracism alerts us to the threat of expulsion from our social group. Like any threat to the organism, the threat of social exclusion from mobbing activates the fight/flight/freeze responses.[13] Threats prime us for action, as when we prepare to either fight or flee. When the situation seems hopeless and we are overwhelmed by helplessness we respond by freezing, doing nothing, in the face of a significant threat to our life or to our identity. Mobbing is a threat to social survival that can activate any of the fight, flight, or freeze responses. Understanding the overlap between physical and social pain provides insight into how primal a need belonging is and how deep the resulting injury from social exclusion and ostracism.

The experience of rejection by significant others in workplace mobbing causes emotional and, often, real physical pain and results in increased monitoring in future relationships in order to protect against the pain of a repeat experience of ostracism. In our clinical and consulting work, mobbing victims often talk about their heightened sensitivity post-mobbing, in both work and social relationships, to social cues that indicate distancing and rejection. Mobbing victims are on the lookout for signs that they will be rejected again. This heightened vigilance to cues of potential rejection and exclusion is self-protective. Having been ostracized and humiliated, mobbing victims are understandably cautious about reentering the workplace, even if they have the opportunity to do so. They don't want to experience that kind of pain again.

Ostracism is a profound humiliation because it segregates victims from the groups to which they have been aligned and from which they derive meaning. In the workplace, mobbing and ostracism are, by their nature, public acts. The visibility of the mobbed and marginalized victim compounds the injury and humiliation. The severed work connections that result from mobbing also cut a victim off from access to informal networks of work support, information about other jobs in one's field, and the second- and third-degree work connections that often lead to job opportunities. Being ostracized holds a victim back both emotionally and in practical, concrete ways that make it much harder to pick up the pieces and move forward.

The body and brain read the events of a mobbing as threats to one's integrity—which they indeed are—and can respond by activating the fight response—a defensive and sometimes aggressive reaction. With the body and brain interpreting exclusion as a threat to belonging and, therefore, survival, the ostracized person moves into panic mode and responds similarly to a person experiencing physical pain, including acting aggressively.[5,14] Understand that aggressive responses range from the private subjective experience of anger to violence against others and include a host of intermediate responses such as verbalizing anger and outrage. The following list gives examples of the kinds of humiliation and ostracism, often public, that frequently occur in workplace mobbings and can lead to aggressive responses.

- Being fired or terminated
- Being demoted
- Being publicly criticized
- Being falsely accused of criminal activity or of behaviors that run counter to one's basic set of values
- Being subjected to hostile investigatory procedures
- Being given a negative job reference after termination
- Being refused a job reference after termination

Having read this list, some are likely to think, "What's the big deal?" or "People get fired all the time," or "Just get over it and move on." Those kinds of reactions are more common among people who have *not* been ostracized through mobbing and who therefore do not experientially understand what it's like to be mobbed. Downplaying, minimizing, and discounting the intensity and severity of a victim's experience of workplace mobbing occur when there is an empathy gap. In the context of workplace mobbing, empathy gaps are underestimations of the severity of a person's social pain by another who has not had a similar experience. The notion that to fully grasp and appreciate the intensity or severity of someone's social pain requires having experienced it is the compelling finding of recent research in social psychology.[2] This finding goes some distance toward explaining the insensitivity and even callousness to the plight of a mobbing victim by others in an organization. Those who haven't been mobbed have a much harder time understanding the effects than do those who have been mobbed.

The question for victims trying to heal from mobbing is how this knowledge about social pain and exclusion can help to make decisions that promote recovery. To start with, let's consider the fight/flight/freeze responses that get activated by a person (and most organisms) when they perceive they are under threat, as in the case of the threat of ostracism and social exclusion from mobbing, and how those responses might play out for a mobbing victim.

The Fight Response and Recovery

Defending oneself verbally and in writing against the array of accusations that have been leveled against one in a mobbing; spending time and resources trying to set the record straight and clear one's name; complaining to management or to HR; filing grievances, Equal Employment Opportunity Commission complaints, and lawsuits are all examples of fighting back in a mobbing. None of these are irrational or negative responses to having been mobbed. In some situations these and similar actions may mitigate the impact of the mobbing and even provide some way of clearing one's name. In other situations, these kinds of actions may boomerang and cause even further harm. In deciding whether to fight back or not here are some important considerations.

Standing Up to Mobbing: Some Points to Consider

- By mobbing you, your organization has already demonstrated its willingness to play dirty. Unless you have some real basis for believing that your organization will reexamine its actions toward you and behave more reasonably and honorably, it probably won't. It is more likely to just ramp up its efforts to get rid of you. Nonetheless, it may well be worth trying to have your situation heard by someone in the organization with the power to do something about it.
- No matter how cash strapped your organization may be, it is almost always much wealthier than you and much more prepared to do battle legally than you are and to hang in for a much longer and costlier amount of time.
- There is a huge asymmetry of power when an individual organizational member decides to take on the organization in whatever context. This power imbalance doesn't mean that you shouldn't fight back, but it does mean that you need to know what you are getting yourself into.
- Therefore, it's essential that if you decide to fight back you set "fight" rules for yourself.

  - You can't go this alone. Fighting back is stressful, and you need to know that you have support from family or friends that you can really count on. There are likely to be some dark days ahead.
  - Set a limit on the amount of time and resources that you are willing and able to commit to fighting back. Adhere strictly to those limits. Know when to cut your losses and walk away.
  - Don't make fighting the organization that mobbed you your next career. It isn't worth it. You can quickly use up all your financial and psychological resources trying to fight the organization in order to

prove that you were not as they have portrayed you. More than a few mobbing victims have expended all their resources trying to clear their names and have lost everything including their lives.[15,16,17] Unequivocally, your organization is not worth this level of sacrifice.

The Flight Response and Recovery

Flight is a common response to being mobbed when the victim is still in the workplace. It manifests as increased sick leave, medical leaves of absence, keeping a low profile, hiding out in one's office or in some other location in the workplace, job disengagement, and actively trying to find another job. If it's possible for a mobbing victim to read the writing on the wall early enough and get out of the organization by finding another job before being terminated or feeling that there is no alternative but to quit, then taking the other job is probably a very good move both for one's health and career. Because mobbing victims are so bewildered and wronged by the abusive acts involved in the mobbing, they don't always see what's happening early enough to make a job move. When they finally do see what's happening, they see the events as so unfair and unjust that they often believe they will be vindicated and the mobbing resolved in their favor. Of course, this usually doesn't happen, and the mobbing and destructiveness continue.

At some point, remaining on the job becomes psychologically and emotionally impossible, in spite of the losses involved in leaving. It's when mobbing victims realize they can no longer tolerate the abuse and the ostracism that they make the decision to quit. Quitting under these circumstances is constructive discharge. When working conditions become so unfair, hostile, and intolerable that continuing on in the job is not possible, then quitting is the only reasonable choice. Flight by quitting a workplace where one is being mobbed is a good choice in terms of trying to contain the damage that has already been done and creating a context for healing and recovery. Flight by quitting carries its own high price. The mobbing victim is often frustrated that the organization was never held to account, and the future may seem precarious and uncertain. Nonetheless, quitting is a viable way of cutting one's losses in a mobbing even though it is precisely what the organization wants. At some point, however, it is the victim who must take care of his or her own health and well-being above all else and doing so may mean quitting—often with all of the associated loose ends and negative portrayals left hanging.

The Freeze Response and Recovery

When the options of fighting back and quitting are both perceived as highly undesirable by the mobbing victim, freeze is a likely response. In a mobbing situation, freeze results in doing nothing while experiencing an overwhelming sense of powerlessness and dread.[10] In a freeze response, fighting back takes energy reserves that the mobbing victim no longer has at his or her disposal. Quitting is an equally unpalatable option because the mobbing victim has to make a living and believes that the organization will do everything in its power to prevent that from happening should he or she quit. After all, to stay congruent with the mobbing the organization has to keep the narrative going of the mobbing victim as flawed and troublesome and that means the negative portrayals of the victim must continue. The mobbing victim in freeze mode believes that either no references or bad ones will be all that is forthcoming from the organization and that all of his or her prior history of commitment to the organization will be lost forever. In a state of freeze, the mobbing victim is not able to make a proactive decision to remain in the organization and try to fight back against the negative characterizations or to make the decision to quit and, instead, remains in a state of psychological fear and paralysis. This frozen state is the most precarious of all for a mobbing victim and indicates a need for immediate help and support.

Understand that the experience of being mobbed and the profound humiliation associated with it leaves identifiable traces, signifiers of its presence, in your brain and body.[10,18,19,20] This understanding may help you to be more self-compassionate when the experience feels raw and as if it just happened. Whether to fight back or to flee an organization in which you have been mobbed is an important decision that needs to be made with as much thought and reflection as possible given the difficult context in which you find yourself. Each option has pros and cons associated with it. Freezing, being unable to decide among any possible courses of action, is an indicator that social support and professional help is urgently needed.

Rebuilding Social Support

Social support from family and friends buffers all kinds of difficult periods and experiences in a person's life. Knowing that in spite of how difficult something is, or how damaging, there are one or two or a few people who believe in you and who are prepared to stand by you over the long haul can make the difference between hope and despair and even between life and death. This kind of social support is critical for people who have suffered all kinds of losses and hurts in life, but for a variety of reasons, it is not always available to mobbing victims.

Coworkers typically back away and distance themselves from the mobbing victim as we have already described. The mobbing victim is likely to feel betrayed, left bereft of support at work, and will suffer the loss of the comfort and familiarity of those work connections and relationships. Coworkers whom they counted as friends routinely betray mobbing victims. If the mobbing victim socialized with coworkers and counted them as close friends, the injury resulting from the betrayal will be the most severe. Being betrayed during a mobbing by coworkers whom the mobbing victim once counted as close friends is an example of high betrayal trauma. High betrayal trauma is associated with the most severe, complicated, and long-lasting traumatic symptoms and related mental health problems.[21] Even if the mobbing victim rarely or never socialized outside of work with coworkers who turned against him or her during the mobbing, the victim still suffers the loss of the easy and comfortable work relationships that he or she once enjoyed. Those work relationships were important, and now they are gone. In all likelihood they will never be restored because the betrayal of the victim has been so complete.

Janice Harper, an anthropologist who writes about mobbing, was accused by colleagues and students at the University of Tennessee of trying to get information about uranium so she could build a hydrogen bomb. Harper was subsequently subjected to a Homeland

Security investigation that completely exonerated her. She is unequivocal about the betrayal and loss of coworker friendship and support during a mobbing and says, "Let me be clear: I am not suggesting that if you are being mobbed that those closest to you might betray or hurt you. What I am telling you is that *in almost every case I guarantee they will*—and when they do, they will be the most damaging, and the most committed to your destruction"[22] In a society where the line between work and personal relationships is fuzzy and blurred, the loss of work relationships during a mobbing is devastating.

The goal and hallmark of workplace mobbing is the marginalization and ostracism of the target-victim. In a mobbing, the betrayal of coworkers who were friends succeeds in isolating the mobbing victim during the period of the mobbing and indefinitely afterward. The betrayal and loss of workplace relationships will be constructed by the organization as the victim's fault but is more accurately a function of the organization's recruitment of the victim's coworkers as participants in the mobbing process. After all, those closest in the workplace to the victim know the most and are therefore in the best position to be turned—to use what they know to help in the humiliation and degradation of the victim. In an almost comical understatement, an attorney during litigation subsequent to a workplace mobbing tried warning off a victim by telling him that his coworkers were not his friends. Meynell calls the subversive process of mobbing a "mini-holocaust";[23] Harper calls it "gentle genocide."[22]

But more than most, mobbing victims do need friends, and they absolutely need social support. With work friends usually out of the picture, mobbing victims need to think about rebuilding their network of friendships and social relationships. The question is how and where to do it. We recommend looking to rebuild social relationships in settings and contexts that are novel for the particular mobbing victim. What does this mean? It means going to places and participating in activities that are new for the mobbing victim but that had always featured somewhere on the mobbing victim's wish list or bucket list of things to do. For example, if the mobbing victim had always wanted to learn a new language, now is the time to sign up for classes at a local language school or college or university. Or if learning to paint, or write, or cook, or do ballroom dancing was somewhere on the victim's wish list, now is the time to make the commitment to doing something new in a group with new people.

The purpose isn't to make new friends. Developing new friendships takes time, and mobbing victims are well advised to go slow because of the betrayal of trust that they have experienced. The purpose is to counter the isolation and humiliation of social exclusion and to begin to be a part of a group again, to be doing something meaningful together with others over time on a regular basis. The fact that the activity is new for the mobbing victim means that there are fewer preconceptions about what the experience will be like that the victim brings to the activity and that could reduce the level of participation. The mobbing victim can simply enjoy being greeted in a different language or focusing on the steps in the foxtrot or chopping vegetables with her cooking partner. She can also enjoy the experience of being missed if she is unable to get to a class or group meeting. Such activities provide the experience of belonging and being part of a group without the pressure of intimacy and self-disclosure that is a part of close friendships.

Medical Care, Psychotherapy, and Career Coaching

A chronic intense stressor like workplace mobbing is associated with negative mental and physical health effects that frequently require professional assistance to ameliorate. Our basic recommendation is that you consult with medical and psychotherapeutic professionals who are knowledgeable about the nature of mobbing and its effects. If your health care provider is not familiar with mobbing, then you can provide the necessary background and education by giving your provider journal articles and books that describe what mobbing is, how it proceeds, how long it lasts, and its physical and psychological health effects.

A number of people who have been in contact with us and who have experienced the negative effects of mobbing have given such educational material to their health care providers who, in turn, have been appreciative of the information and have used it to provide better care for them and other patients. A big concern of mobbing victims who know they need professional help to recover is the lack of awareness by their health care providers of what mobbing is and what its health effects are. Such victims understandably fear being misdiagnosed, for example being labeled as paranoid[24] and being provided psychological treatment by a practitioner uninformed about either mobbing or trauma. Because of the physical health consequences associated with mobbing,[13] medical evaluations of workplace mobbing victims should always include assessment of gastrointestinal disturbances, sleep problems, and specific cardiovascular assessment. A sensitive and informed physician is often one of the first to advise a patient who has been mobbed to consider a medical leave of absence because of the negative health impact.

Mobbing victims wisely fear uninformed practitioners because of the risk of revictimization. Victims of workplace mobbing cannot afford the risk of revictimization at the hands of therapists and other health care providers uninformed about mobbing and trauma. For workplace mobbing victims, revictimization means blaming the victim for the trauma, inappropriately labeling or pathologizing the victim, and placing responsibility for resolving the workplace problems on the victim. In order to trust their health care providers to do the best for them, mobbing victims need to know that their providers understand what workplace mobbing is all about.

There is growing awareness in the physical and mental health care communities that trauma is common rather than rare and that trauma can affect multiple domains of a person's life and affect overall functioning and well-being. As a result, an approach known as "trauma-informed care"[1,25] has been developed to provide patients impacted by trauma with integrated physical and mental health care informed by a deep understanding of the nature of trauma and its effects. Trauma-informed medical and psychotherapeutic care for victims of workplace mobbing will recognize that workplace mobbing is a form of interpersonal abuse and acknowledge that mobbing negatively impacts multiple life domains including work and career, relationships with family and friends, beliefs about the self and the world, and the overall sense of identity and self of a mobbing victim.

It is important that mobbing victims select psychotherapists who are aware of the problem of workplace mobbing and who practice trauma-informed therapy. Trauma-informed therapy is not a specific type of psychotherapy—many psychotherapeutic approaches can be trauma-informed. Workplace mobbing is a potentially life-altering experience that can affect all aspects of victims' lives, from their relationships to their current and future work to their identities and very sense of self. Because of the nature of trauma, especially of interpersonal trauma like workplace mobbing, power dynamics are always in play. Mobbing didn't just happen out of the blue to a particular person in a particular organization; much larger cultural and organizational power dynamics are always involved and relate to the process of targeting someone who is different from the dominant group or whose identity has been constructed to be that of a villain or a bad apple that needs to be removed.

Trauma-informed therapy is the treatment model most likely to include an explicit focus on examination of the organizational and cultural features involved in the victim's experience of being mobbed and on an analysis of the associated power dynamics. For the victim and victim's family a full understanding of these power dynamics is essential for recovery. Trauma-informed psychotherapists are those most likely to place an understanding of trauma and its effects at the center of their practice and to provide a welcoming and hospitable context within which victims can do the work of recovery while minimizing the risks of revictimization from lack of knowledge and understanding.[1,25] For victims of mobbing, we strongly recommend physical and mental health care that is trauma-informed and sensitive.

Career coaching can be useful for those who have been mobbed and who now must explore their options for continuing their work and careers. Effective career coaching and counseling for mobbing victims should also be trauma-informed, and the career coach should understand that decisions about remaining in the workplace, leaving the workplace, or picking up the pieces after being terminated from the workplace have been complicated by the trauma of ongoing abuse at work. The mobbing victim's sense of self and sense of work or professional identity typically have been damaged by the mobbing experience. As a result, career coaching, especially at the beginning, may go a lot slower than is usual. The usual career goal-setting process will be longer and slower and should be broken down into smaller increments with which the mobbing victim can cope. For example, a trauma-informed career coach will spend as much time as needed helping the mobbing victim-client to identify what needs to happen before he or she is able to start the goal-setting process. It's a difference that makes all the difference. Trauma-informed career coaches can be invaluable in helping a mobbing victim assess their job-related resources and strengths and recover belief in their skills, expertise, and competence. Conversely, career coaches who are not trauma-informed and who do not understand workplace mobbing and its destructive effects can end up doing more harm than good.

For both psychotherapy and career coaching any suggestion from the therapist or coach that it is time to "move on" or to "get over it" should be a red flag warning the mobbing victim that the therapist or coach does not have an adequate understanding of the centrality of trauma and its effects on a person's life. Paradoxically, the path to a robust and secure recovery from mobbing involves recognizing, exploring, and accepting its damaging and traumatic effects.

Reclaiming Personal Agency by Telling the Story of Being Mobbed

There is a basic reason why telling your story of being mobbed is important. During the mobbing, your story—the story of who you are as a person and as a coworker—was hijacked by the participants in the mobbing and by the organization in which you worked. Those key players appropriated your story and portrayed you in as negative a way as possible in order to get rid of you. You were mischaracterized, and pieces of information about you were distorted and used to construct this negative portrayal. That's what happens in every mobbing. Much as you may have tried, you were not able to get your organization to issue a correction, so to speak, and to set things right by correcting the gossip, innuendo, misinformation, and false information that was distributed about you and used to bring you down. During the mobbing, your story was maliciously re-authored by the participants in the mobbing. It is important to reclaim your story of who you are as a person and as a coworker. You do that by telling the story of being mobbed your way and in your own time to people to whom you wish to tell it.

Telling your story of being mobbed allows you to set the record straight from your perspective and to get your version of the events of the mobbing in circulation. Telling your story has the secondary benefit of helping you to fill in the gaps and to develop a coherent account of what happened. Recovery from trauma is directly linked to the ability to develop an organized and articulate narrative of traumatic events and the meanings that you have come to assign to those events.[26,27,28,29] Over time those meanings may change and become more nuanced, but the more they are embedded in a structured and consistent account of what happened and how those events impacted you and what they meant to you, the stronger and more robust your recovery is likely to be.[10,11] Telling the story of your mobbing also requires you to stand up to the embarrassment and shame of the whole experience, to investigate the sources of that embarrassment and shame, and ultimately to cast those feelings off. Telling your story doesn't mean that you are going public with it, although you could. It simply means that you are taking your story back, not leaving it to those who participated in humiliating and vilifying you to tell the details of who you are as a person and as a coworker. You might start by telling the story to yourself by writing it down, then branch out to telling the story to those closest to you and outward from there as your preferences guide you. Telling your story your way is your right, and after the trauma of mobbing it is a major step toward reclaiming your autonomy and authorship of your own life.

Attending to Relationships and Life Commitments beyond Work

Work can get in the way of other life commitments and sources of meaning. Family and friends, creative and leisure activities, and helping others can get pushed to the side by the demands of work. But those life commitments and sources of meaning are especially important for mobbing victims because they are not dependent on work. In the wake of mobbing, refocusing on important relationships, creative and leisure activities, and on helping others can provide meaning and a sense of purpose in life and offer small but significant daily pleasure and satisfaction. Recommending relaxation and involvement in creative and leisure activities may seem too simple at first glance. But such activities are vital in helping the body to assimilate the effects of trauma from workplace mobbing. These kinds of activities and the positive social interactions that go along with them are important for integrating traumatic events in the body and brain and for helping to situate the trauma in the past rather than in the present.[18]

It's important for mobbing victims to look around and see who has stood by them during the stressful weeks, months, and sometimes years of the mobbing. Family members and friends may have offered support and friendship in different ways, but for mobbing victims there will be no doubt about who has stood by them and who has not. Refocusing on those relationships that have endured and nurturing and appreciating them is both satisfying and helpful. Likewise, creative and leisure activities present opportunities for doing things that take effort, require focus, and are enjoyable and productive. The value of creative and leisure activities in recovery from mobbing should not be underestimated, and time set aside for these activities is time well spent.

Helping others can also become an important source of meaning and focus for mobbing victims. In addition to the hundreds of ways that a person can help others, mobbing victims can make a unique contribution by helping other mobbing victims. A person who has been victimized by workplace mobbing is unlikely to have an empathy gap that leads them to discount the intensity and pain of others who have endured workplace mobbings. Many mobbing victims have become involved in helping others who like them have been mobbed. Some have helped others by telling their personal story, others by writing about mobbing or making documentary films. Still others have helped by setting up websites where people who have been mobbed and people who work to prevent mobbing can come together. Others help by being a compassionate witness and listener. When balanced by appropriate self-care, helping others, especially other mobbing victims, can return meaning and a sense of connectedness to a mobbing victim's life.

Reengagement as an Indicator of Recovery

Workplace mobbing interrupts not just your career trajectory but your hopes and dreams for your job in the organization in which you were mobbed. More than likely you were committed to your job and planned to continue to make meaningful contributions to your organization. Mobbing stopped all of that. It thwarted both your short-term goals for your job and career within your organization and your long-term goals for career development. For example, as a nurse manager in a cancer hospital you loved your job and felt you were making important contributions to your organization and the overall quality of patient care. You also believed that the mentoring and burn-out prevention systems you had set up for the nurses at the hospital contributed to lower turnover rates, a high rate of job satisfaction, and increased overall well-being. The surveys and statistics that the hospital collected supported your belief that these programs were effective.

That you were viciously mobbed in this hospital you had loved and to which you had devoted so much energy was a shattering and life-altering experience for you. You grieved; you sought medical care and psychotherapy. You gathered your family and friends close to you and let them know that you needed and appreciated them. You heard about a few other nurses who had been mobbed, and you started to communicate with them on the Internet. You were beginning to tell your story to others. In one way or another, over time, you had followed the principles for mobbing recovery described in this chapter. In the process, what you also understood was that there were some goals that were no longer attainable for you. For example, the career goals that you had developed at the hospital where you were mobbed were not going to be realized there. Slowly, though, you were beginning to set new goals for yourself that you dared to hope were attainable elsewhere.

After workplace mobbing, an indicator of recovery is the degree to which a victim is able to reengage with life and find meaning and purpose in relationships and in creative, leisure, and service activities. Setting new job and career goals is also an indicator of reengagement but may trail behind meaningful involvement in relationships and other activities. For workplace mobbing victims, reengagement in life first requires disengagement from goals that are no longer attainable, such as building programs and being promoted in the organization in which one was mobbed. This process of disengagement from activities that are no longer possible and goals that are no longer attainable and reengagement with relationships and activities and alternative career goals takes time but is an important and useful way of marking recovery.

Recovery Takes Time

Recovery from mobbing proceeds at its own pace and doesn't move forward in a smooth and linear way. There are stops and starts, and recovery is more like a back and forth movement over time. Some days are better than others. Because workplace mobbing is such a totalizing experience and affects so many domains of a person's life and functioning, it is no surprise that recovery can be slow. Patience is the order of the day for both the victim of mobbing and those who love and care about the victim. Along with patience, self-compassion is also important and can be very easy to overlook. Mobbing victims have been through the proverbial mill, and it's not uncommon for them to see themselves not only as victims but also as failures. Self-compassion helps mobbing victims to step back and look at themselves in the same way that they might look at someone whom they cared deeply about who had gone through the same experiences they had. Mobbing victims who practice self-compassion can bring the same caring, nonjudgmental, and supportive presence to themselves that they most assuredly would bring to someone whom they loved. The paradoxical relationship between acceptance and change, or recovery in the case of mobbing victims, is expressed by Rodney Donaldson in this way: "Our very notions of 'change' change. Paradoxically, we find that we change, not by trying to be some image of self different from who we are, but precisely by accepting who we are—and then finding ourselves changed by virtue of having undergone that acceptance."[30]

If You Are the Target-Victim: Some Guidelines for What to Do in an Ongoing Mobbing[13]

Establish Physical and Interpersonal Safe Zones at Work

- Identify spaces in which you can be physically and emotionally safe. If there are no such places, consider sick leave or another leave of absence.

Recall, Describe, and Document Critical Events in the Mobbing: Build Coherent Narratives

- Tell the story of the events of the mobbing, at your own pace, to a trusted family member or friend.

- Collect emails, memos, reprimands, disciplinary actions, evaluations, and any other documentary materials relating to the mobbing.
- Log, journal, or document as much detail about the events as you can. This record will help you to fill in the gaps later should you have difficulty in recall. It will also help in therapies, such as exposure therapy, that have demonstrated effectiveness in trauma recovery work.
- The documentary materials and log or journal will also be helpful should you decide to pursue grievances, regulatory complaints, or lawsuits.
- Give copies of all materials to a trusted family member or friend for safekeeping. This is important because you might find yourself wanting to throw out all signs and symbols of the mobbing in order to feel free of it.

Assess Physical, Emotional, and Behavioral Responses to the Mobbing

- Obtain a medical examination and include a cardiology checkup in the exam. Tell your health care provider what is happening at work. Bring this book, chart, or other literature about mobbing with you so that your health care provider will have resource information about mobbing. This resource information will help health care providers to avoid harmful misdiagnoses.
- Pay attention to the feelings, sensations, and experiences that you are having in your body. Notice how your body feels when you are tense and stressed. Notice how your body feels when you are relaxed and what is different in your body between states of tension and states of relaxation. Encourage relaxation.
- Reflect on your own emotional and behavioral responses to the mobbing. Try to identify how you are responding and what you are doing both at work and at home that is helpful and/or unhelpful. Ask a trusted

family member or friend to help you in this process. Go at your own pace. Do more of what is helpful.

- Evaluate whether any of your responses have made a difference in improving the situation at work. If any have, continue those actions that have been helpful.
- Identify any strong or overwhelming feelings of sadness, anger, despair, or desire to lash back at the perpetrators. Share these feelings with a trusted family member or friend. Seek immediate professional help.

Obtain Knowledgeable Professional Help as Needed

- Mental health professional with knowledge of both trauma and mobbing.
- Couples or family therapist.
- Career counselor or career coach.
- Attorney specializing in employment law for employees.

Make Self-Care a Priority

- Rest and relaxation.
- Nutrition.
- Exercise.
- Spiritual practices, meditation, breathing.

Review Informal Options for Resolving the Mobbing

- Meet with supervisor or management representative (not someone you believe to be involved in the mobbing).
- Describe in detail the abusive, unfair, and unethical behaviors to which you are being subjected as clearly and concisely as possible. This option requires careful preparation that includes review of documents you have collected or developed.
- Think carefully about what changes in your current work context would potentially resolve the mobbing.

For example, transfer to a different department,
assignment to a different supervisor, recision of demotion
and reinstatement to previous job, clarification of
job description and responsibilities, more resources
with which to carry out your job, notification to key
participants in the mobbing to immediately cease and
desist their abusive and unfair behaviors toward you,
management and staff training about mobbing, and so on.

- Respectfully request all changes that you believe
are necessary and that have the potential to end the
mobbing and restore dignity to you.

Review Formal Options for Resolving the Mobbing

- Organizational conflict resolution procedures.
Mobbing causes an imbalance of power in which
the target-victim has considerably less power than
the participants in the mobbing, irrespective of
organizational rank. Therefore, be cautious of mediation
procedures that involve you in direct mediation with
the mobbers; it is possible that more harm than good
can come out of it.
- Internal grievance.
- External grievance.
- Regulatory complaints.
- Lawsuits.

Review Options for Staying or Exiting the Organization

- Remain and seek redress.
- Remain and not seek redress.
- Exit and seek redress.
- Exit and not seek redress.

Accept and Grieve Losses from Mobbing

- Acknowledge losses and associated feelings.
- Express feelings about losses to trusted family member
or friend.

Reaffirm Values by Which You Wish to Live

- Identify beliefs and values that have provided strength and hope throughout the mobbing.
- Foster self-compassion.
- Foster empathy and compassion for others.
- Acknowledge life's uncertainties and unfairness.
- Reclaim belief in self.
- Appreciate the presence of those who have stood by you and supported you throughout the mobbing.

Engage in Meaningful Life Activities

- Develop new interests and reengage with old interests.
- Develop new skills and brush up on old ones.
- Care and nourish trusting relationships.
- Do something creative.
- Experience laughter, fun, and pleasure.
- Set realistic goals and begin to work toward attaining them.
- Project yourself into a positive and satisfying future.

Support for Family Members of Employees

- Obtain accurate information about mobbing and its effects on victims.
- Obtain accurate information about legal rights.
- Know that recovery for mobbing victims is attainable with support.
- Practice self-care.

Conclusion

Recovery is possible for mobbing victims and should be a primary goal. Because mobbing affects work and occupational identity and then spirals out and encompasses multiple other aspects of a person's life, recovery can be slow and complicated. Those who have not experienced the social pain of a mobbing may understandably find it difficult to relate to the intensity and hopelessness that many mobbing victims feel. We hope that we have shed light on the empathy gaps that prevent those who have not been mobbed from more fully appreciating the experience of those who have been mobbed and, in so doing, have helped both groups to understand the distance between them and, ultimately, to close that gap.

Mobbing victims cannot fully recover without the social support and contact of those who have stood by them. Those relationships are critical. Equally important are the new relationships developed by mobbing victims as they participate in creative, leisure, and service activities that are part of their reengagement with the social world. But reengagement also suggests the difficult process of disengagement that mobbing victims must also go through. Letting go of commitments and goals that are no longer feasible because of the workplace mobbing can be a difficult and painful process. The truth about almost all mobbing victims is that they loved their work and valued the organizations within which they did that work. Recovery is about reclaiming the right and ability to work again, to enjoy relationships again, and to participate fully in the world again.

Mobbing Recovery Tools

I F YOU ARE READING THIS CHAPTER YOU OR SOMEONE you know and care about has probably already survived mobbing. Perhaps you are looking for tools to help yourself or the person you care about who has been mobbed. Or, you are a family member or close friend of the mobbing victim, have experienced secondary victimization as a result of their mobbing, and are looking for help for yourself. This chapter is designed to be read and used in conjunction with the previous chapter, "Recovering from Mobbing." Together, these two chapters provide information about the principles and process of recovery from mobbing and tools to help you and those you care about make thoughtful decisions about how best to move forward in the recovery process.

As we have already discussed, mobbing is associated with multiple losses in multiple domains of life, making it a tough experience to undergo. People who have been mobbed make use of information about mobbing in different ways based on their own experiences and individual reactions. From the many people who have contacted us about their mobbing experiences since we first started writing about it, we know that some felt relieved and validated to learn that what they had gone through actually had a name. They held on to our previous book and articles and shared them with important others in their lives. What they were reading about mobbing confirmed their experiences, helped give them a context for understanding what had happened to them, and also confirmed that their experiences were "real" and that they were not losing their grip on reality. Others had no idea that a research community devoted to the study of mobbing even existed, and they set about reading everything they could get their hands on about it.

Still others felt validated by what they read about mobbing but could not tolerate reading more than a few paragraphs at a time without being overwhelmed once again by the feelings of dread, anxiety, fear, and helplessness that were so much a part of their primary experience of being mobbed. For them, reading about mobbing was crucially important but needed to occur over a longer period of time so that their reading and learning could be accomplished in emotionally manageable chunks. Yet others described getting our previous book, wanting the affirmation the book provided, putting it on their bedside table, but not being ready to read it at all because they feared being overwhelmed by a flood of terrible memories and feelings about being mobbed. For this group, our previous book and other writings about mobbing held the promise of future help and greater understanding. Individuals in this group did not feel able to cope with the memories and emotions that they feared would be triggered by starting to read about mobbing. They needed to wait. Each of these examples of how mobbing victims utilized information about mobbing suggests that the individuals were at different places in their recovery processes and had different needs.

As we stated in the preface, we intend this self-help book to be trauma-informed. In keeping with the trauma-informed model,[1,2] this chapter provides tools that are designed to build new skills and deepen understandings of what happened during and after mobbing. We have developed a number of tools based on our work with target-victims of workplace mobbing that incorporate trauma-informed best practices. These tools and skills are designed to help people develop new understandings about mobbing and its impact and to think about what is best for them, as unique individuals, in the recovery process. The tools and skills are also designed to increase choice by encouraging brainstorming and the envisioning of as many preferred future scenarios as possible. Deepening understandings, developing skills, and increasing choice are all basic elements of the trauma-informed model.

Research on workplace mobbing is still very young, dating back to the work of Heinz Leymann in the 1980s.[3,4,5] Much of the work that has been done since then focuses on identifying and conceptualizing the social process of mobbing and on understanding the effects of mobbing on target-victims and bystanders, and to a lesser extent on family members. Recovery strategies are now only beginning to be addressed for those who have been mobbed and for their families. This book focuses on healing and recovering from workplace mobbing. It is a contribution to the body of knowledge about recovery strategies and is derived from our backgrounds as mental health clinicians and our clinical and consulting work with mobbing victims and their families. We have developed the recovery tools provided in this chapter based on our work with workplace mobbing victims, and on the trauma-informed model of health care,[1,2,6] social exclusion theory,[7,8,9] and practices in narrative therapy.[10,11,12]

However, we do want to remind readers that use of these tools to help in recovery from mobbing does not replace professional mental health care and that obtaining professional mental health care is one of the 10 principles for recovery we discussed in chapter 7. If using the mobbing recovery tools in this chapter and completing the reflective activities associated with them cause increased emotional distress, then these activities should be stopped and resumed at another time when they do not cause increased emotional distress or they should be completed while working with a mental health care provider.

The recovery tools in this chapter also focus attention on what happened to a victim during and after mobbing and on the importance of tracking those effects and losses. In keeping with trauma-informed best practices,[1,2,6] our focus throughout this book and especially in this chapter is on what happened to the victim of workplace mobbing rather than on what is wrong with the victim. In fact, we don't assume that there is anything wrong with the victim at all. In this chapter, we also provide tools that the victim and his or her family can use to help them go on with their lives as productively as possible while not minimizing the severity of the injuries done to them. Indeed, the recovery tools presented here are designed to help the victim and his or her family address the question of how to go on after the trauma of workplace mobbing.

Your Mobbing Recovery Support Team

In terms of practical tools, you might be wondering why we focus first on organizing your mobbing recovery support team. The answer to that question is both simple and profound. The result of workplace mobbing is social exclusion, ostracism, and elimination from the workplace itself or from a unit within it. As we have already described in previous chapters, the effects of social exclusion are deeply painful psychologically and even physically. They rip you from your moorings as a member of a social group and call into question your worthiness to be a member of that group. Social exclusion is humiliating and represents a deep injury to your core identity as a human and as a social being that radiates outward and affects multiple domains of your life. Transcending the identity injuries to one's status as a valued member of a workgroup requires connecting with trusting and caring others. Hence our focus on identifying safe and trustworthy social support first.

Workplace mobbing victims, by definition, have been betrayed by coworkers whom they previously trusted and cared about. Understandably, they are likely to be less trusting and more suspicious of future relationships. Having been burned by betrayals in a mobbing puts victims on guard and in a self-protective mode. They don't want to be burned again by further betrayals. For mobbing victims, choosing to trust others again is frightening and risky. Yet, recovery and healing from mobbing ultimately require involvement with caring others. The challenge for mobbing victims is how to decide whom to trust so that their psychological safety is protected.

Ruptures, however, are a predictable part of all relationships, even the best of relationships.[13] The most important part of being in relationships with others who are important to us, whether personally or professionally, is knowing how to participate in the work of relationship repair when ruptures occur, as they inevitably will. In both our work lives and our personal lives we are most likely to trust those who are willing to work on repairing relationship ruptures instead of ignoring them and pretending they don't matter. So for those whose trust and friendships have been violated by the betrayals of workplace mobbing, deciding whom to risk trusting again has far-reaching implications.

Placing Trust in Others

In our personal relationships, we are most likely to trust others who:

- Are caring and nonjudgmental
- Know how to listen and respond
- Have stood by us in difficult times
- Tell the truth as they see it to us and to others
- Let us know that they want us in their lives
- Hang in and work on repairing the relationship when ruptures occur

In our relationships with professionals, including health care providers, we are most likely to trust others who:

- Are professionally competent
- Treat us with respect and interest
- Assume a collaborative rather than expert stance
- Help us to tap into our own resources
- Instill confidence and hope

Tool #1, "Who Do You Need on Your Mobbing Recovery Support Team: Gathering the Team Together," shown in Figure 8.1, is a simple tool for thinking about who in your life should be part of your mobbing recovery support team. The tool lists people, both personal and professional, who are likely to be important and helpful to you as you go on with your life post-mobbing and who you will want or need to go with you as you go forward. The list is not designed as a checklist. It is designed to encourage broad-based thinking about people in your life who either have already supported you, or who could in the future. There is no one specific person from any category on the list who must be included in a mobbing recovery support team. Everyone is different, and everyone's relationship history is unique.

But you will need both personal and professional relationships to help you recover and transcend the devastating effects of mobbing. No one can recover from mobbing alone, and connecting with others in order to refashion your life after mobbing is itself a way of carrying on. When you invite others into your life you are resisting the outcome of social exclusion and ostracism that was assigned to you by those who participated in your mobbing. The people who you eventually gather together become an informal support network. All of them may not know each other. What's important is that you know who they are and how they can support you as you go on with your life.

To use the tool, reflect on each category and determine whether there is someone in that category who already is actively supporting you or who would be likely to do so in some way, either directly or indirectly. Developing a social support network after mobbing is not so much about telling others the details of your experiences of being mobbed—although it could be—as it is about "peopling" your life again with others with whom you feel comfortable and safe. For example, with some in the "friends" category the benefit is simply being with them and sharing a cup of coffee or watching a movie. Not everyone in your social support network needs to know all of the details about what happened to you or even any of the details. Such disclosure decisions are made and revised over time. It is the presence of caring others in your life that is most important—not what they know about the mobbing.

When thinking about who might be a part of your mobbing recovery support network, cast the net as wide as possible but make your own sense of psychological safety the priority. Share information about the details of the mobbing and its effects on you and your family only to the extent that you feel safe and comfortable. Take your time and think through each decision. As for the professionals you invite into your mobbing recovery network, their professional roles will determine the kind and amount of information that is necessary for them to know in order to be of help to you. You may also discover that you find members of your mobbing recovery and support network through mobbing and bullying support groups on Facebook and other social media sites. However you do it, putting together a network of social support after mobbing is a form of active resistance against the damaging effects of social exclusion and ostracism and a repudiation of the shame that is so much a part of the experience of being mobbed.

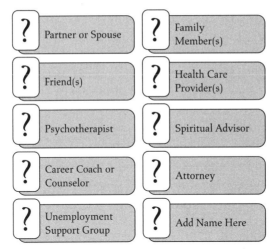

FIGURE 8.1 Tool #1: Who Do You Need on Your Mobbing Recovery Support Team?

Mapping the Effects of Mobbing

In previous chapters we have discussed the damaging effects of mobbing on the victim and on the victim's family and tracked how these effects can reach into every aspect of a person's life and functioning. Tool #2, "How Have I and My Family Been Impacted by Mobbing? Mapping and Tracking the Effects of Mobbing," shown in Figure 8.2, provides a framework for examining the specific ways in which mobbing has impacted the victim's life and that of her or his family and loved ones. Partners, spouses, and other family members can also use the tool to track the effects of mobbing on their lives from their own perspectives. The tool offers a way to zoom in on the following crucial questions:

- How have I been impacted by mobbing?
- How have my family and others whom I love been impacted by mobbing?
- What losses have I suffered?
- Which effects of mobbing on my life require the most urgent attention?

"What's the point of zooming in on the effects of mobbing on my life," you might reasonably ask. "The whole experience has been so devastating and traumatic that it is just too painful to examine in detail the specific ways in which mobbing has wreaked havoc in my life and in the life of my family." These kinds of questions and comments are serious and deserve serious and thoughtful responses.

The experience of powerlessness is a basic feature of mobbing. By the time most workplace mobbing victims realize that they are being ganged up on with the goal of being driven from the workplace, there is little they can do to stop the momentum of the eliminative process well under way. Remember, too, that perpetrators in workplace mobbing commonly attempt to neutralize their victims by keeping them out of key communication and information loops. Being denied adequate and accurate information about what is going on that affects you is one definition of powerlessness and a common aggressive tactic of workplace mobbing perpetrators. Countering powerlessness in mobbing involves the difficult experience of naming and tracking the losses and other effects of mobbing in your life.[10,11,12,14] What is most important to keep in mind, however, is that when you map the suffering and losses that you have experienced as a mobbing victim you are reclaiming your dignity and your power by affirming that you matter—that your life matters, that people you care about matter—and that the pain and losses you have suffered have real effects in the world and that these effects matter.

There are other important reasons for identifying and naming the effects of mobbing in your life. Identifying and naming these effects is a way of rightsizing them—of putting them into perspective. The catchphrase "to name it is to tame it"[15] has been used to illustrate how the process of naming something, especially something overwhelming, is important in reclaiming control.[6,10,11,12,14] Mobbing has multiple negative effects that influence just about every domain of life, but the significance of these effects for each mobbing victim is necessarily going to be different. For a younger person in a high-demand occupation, the impact of mobbing on reemployability and future career prospects is likely to be much less significant than for an older person working in a highly specialized but low-demand job field. Some mobbing victims will be most concerned about the impact of mobbing on their physical or psychological health. For others, the primary concern will be the impact of mobbing on their personal relationships and family lives. Assessing and naming the effects of mobbing rightsizes them by allowing victims and family members to focus first on the areas of their lives most impacted by mobbing, knowing that they can attend to the other effects later.

When we name what troubles us and what is of concern to us we are also, at the same time, naming what we value in life and what our preferences are for how we carry on. A victim, in naming and describing the devastating effects of mobbing on his or her life and family, is in the same breath revealing what he or she would like to have happen instead.[10,11,12] The flip side of what troubles us most in a particular situation is the implicit image of what a desirable situation would look like. Naming the impact of mobbing connects not only to its destructive effects but also, if only implicitly at first, to a vision of what a reclaimed life after mobbing looks like to a victim or family member. A mobbing victim who is troubled by his or her mistrust and suspiciousness of others is at the same time revealing that he or she wants to be involved in mutual and trusting relationships. A family member who is troubled by the emotional distancing of her partner who was mobbed at work is at the same time revealing her desire for closeness and intimacy. The flip side of what troubles and devastates us is what we most want and desire. Naming the effects of mobbing and mapping their impact is an acknowledgment that a victim's experience of loss and injury matter in the world as do their hopes and dreams for a better future.[10,11,12]

Tool #2, "How Have I and My Family Been Impacted by Mobbing? Mapping and Tracking the Effects of Mobbing," includes a list of negative events and impacts from mobbing that are identified in the professional literature.[16] Reflect on each item and decide whether the particular effect from mobbing applies either to you as a victim or to a member of your family or to both. If you are a family member using the tool, then do the same thing, but from your own perspective. If you think the negative effect applies, place a check mark (✓) by the item in the column for "Self" or "Family" or in both columns.

For each checked item, decide how significant the particular effect is on you and/or your family and how important it is to address it. Rank each checked item from 1 to 5, with 5 indicating that the mobbing impact is severe and in need of urgent attention and 1 indicating that the negative effect is present but is of lower priority. Finally, provide a brief narrative describing how the particular negative effect from mobbing has impacted you and/or your family. Using this tool can help you to map the damaging effects of mobbing on you and

Effect	Self	Family	Priority	Brief Description
	(For each applicable item, place a ✔ in one or both columns)		Rank each ✔ item from 1 (lower priority) to 5 (highest priority)	(Provide basic information about each ✔ item)
Job loss				
Demotion				
Reduced income				
Reduced health & retirement benefits				
Reemployment difficulties				
Damage to reputation				
Loss of self-confidence				
Damage to sense of identity				
Loss of belief in the world as fair & just				
Physical health problems				
Psychological health problems				
Relationship conflict				
Family conflict				
Loss of friendships				
Mistrust of others				
Insecurity about the future				
Other				

FIGURE 8.2 Tool #2: How Have I and My Family Been Impacted by Mobbing?
Mapping and Tracking the Effects of Mobbing

your family and to assign priority to those problems that need more immediate attention than others. At the same time, using this tool provides an opening to what a more desirable post-mobbing future might look like since what worries and distresses you also reveals your values, commitments, and preferences.

Getting Your Life Back after Mobbing

Let's make one thing clear. There is nothing good about workplace mobbing. But after being mobbed, people still have their lives to live and they want their lives back. Mobbing robs victims of their lives as they knew them, and understandably, victims want to resume living as fully as they can. In the wake of the losses, injuries, and pain inflicted on a victim by workplace mobbing it is not easy to get one's life back, especially in times of economic recession like these. There is no going back to life before mobbing. Like most interpersonal traumas, mobbing leaves its trace on a victim's body, mind, family life, past, present, and future.[17,18] Like all traumas, there is no resolving mobbing or solving it or dissolving it. But there is moving beyond mobbing, developing life-changing and healing insights from it, becoming a more emotionally attuned survivor of it, and even healing from it. However, there is no forgetting about it and no returning to life as it was before mobbing. That does not mean, however, that life cannot be good again.

Because workplace mobbing changes and rearranges just about everything in a victim's life, one of the things that a victim can do is pay close attention to the changes that have occurred, assess their impact, and consider their meaning. By paying close attention to what has happened as a result of mobbing and to the gentle stirrings of hope for a different and more just future, mobbing can be catalytic. Being mobbed in the workplace is a painful way to learn more about oneself and others, but it is a way to do that. Mobbing can be a catalyst for envisioning a different and preferred future for one's work life and one's life in general. It's possible and probably likely that the values and priorities one held onto before being mobbed have shifted afterward. After being mobbed, changes in values and priorities point to new directions and preferences for one's life.

For example, a woman who was mobbed in higher education and who had previously earned a six-figure income turned down another six-figure-income job a few years later because the new job no longer matched the interests and passions she had developed after being mobbed and forced out of her job. She and her family had learned to make do with a lot less money, and she realized when seriously considering the job offer that she was not willing to compromise her new commitments or her time with her partner and children that she had come to cherish. For this woman and for others who have endured workplace mobbing, the trauma was shaping of her life in ways that she ultimately recognized as promoting growth and increased wisdom. Her values and priorities had changed, and she was moving beyond mobbing with commitments to different kinds of work that deeply satisfied her and afforded her much more time with her partner and family. That she was now paid significantly less and held a position with reduced prestige and status was no longer that important to her. We share this anecdote only to point out that the trauma of mobbing shapes its victims' lives in different and unique ways as they go on in life. This woman's new direction was working for her. We are not suggesting that the same directions or priorities would work for everyone. What we are saying is that it is likely that one's preferences, priorities, and directions in life will change in important ways after mobbing and that what is most profoundly disturbing about having been mobbed is also a signpost for how we wish to work and live in the future.

What Does Your Distress and Suffering Tell You about How You Want to Work and Live?

- What does your suffering and distress from workplace mobbing tell you about what you value most in your career and in your life?
- What do these experiences of suffering and distress tell you about what you want in the future in your career and in your life?
- What does your unwillingness to forget the trauma of workplace mobbing and its impact on you and your family tell you about yourself and what you value?

Tool #3, "How Do I Get My Life Back after Mobbing? Imagining Preferred Scenarios," shown in Figure 8.3, is designed to help mobbing victims and their families figure out what priorities and preferred futures seem most desirable. By completing Tool #2 above, you have already finished the first step. By naming the effects of being mobbed on yourself and your family and identifying the impacts of mobbing that are the highest priority for you, you have begun the process of healing and recovery. Naming how mobbing hurt you and your family is also the first part of telling the story of what happened. The importance of this step cannot be overstated. Mobbing victims commonly face nonresponsiveness and even disdain from others as they attempt to describe what happened and its impact on them and on their families. The telling of the story of being mobbed and its effects is another act of resistance against mobbing—a refusal to be silenced and shamed—even if the telling is to a small number of people only. Naming the effects of mobbing on you and your family and telling the story of how you were mobbed is an affirmation that your experiences and your account of those experiences are important and that they matter.

The second and third steps of Tool #3 involve inviting some of those whom you have included in your mobbing recovery support team (see Tool #1 above) to listen to your story of having been mobbed and to engage in active dialogue with you, over time, about what happened and its impact on you and your family. When you were gathering your mobbing recovery support team, the primary goal was to "people" your life in resistance to the isolation of mobbing. Now the goal is not only to "people" your life but to actively engage with some of them in telling your story of having been mobbed and listening to their responses. Social support and engagement with others is the antithesis of the exclusion and isolation of mobbing and is therefore a central element of recovery in its own right.

In dialogue you are a witness to your own story just as your listening partners are witnesses to your story. As you enter into dialogue with others about your mobbing experiences, your listening partners hear your story, but you also hear yourself telling your own story, and the process of telling and retelling can lead to deeper understandings and richer, more meaningful insights. Stories and meanings are not static. Dialogue allows you to hold your story up to the light, to see facets of the story that you may not have noticed earlier on, and to enhance your understanding of the details of the trauma of being mobbed and its impact and meaning for you and your family.

You have included specific people in your mobbing recovery support team for a reason. Most likely, some are personal family and friend relationships and others are professional relationships. That you have included these people on your mobbing recovery support team means that you value them and want them in your life in some way. Keep in mind that, in general, people are not skilled at listening to trauma stories and prefer to minimize or deny them. But you cannot be healed without the presence of others in your life who know what happened to you. As you tell your story of being mobbed to those on your support team at a time and pace comfortable for you, extend compassion to them and to yourself as they extend compassion back to you. Selected support team members to whom you wish to tell your story of being mobbed need only be good enough listeners—they need not be perfect. It is only through the talk and talk back of dialogue that trust can develop and that stories and meanings, including the story of being mobbed, can be more fully and deeply understood.

The new insights and deepened understandings that are brought about through the process of dialogue[19] about the trauma of mobbing can also give rise to the emergence of new possibilities for your future. As you continue to engage in dialogue with important others about the experience of having been mobbed and the impact that it has had on your life, the image of a more desirable future will begin to take shape. It's important to pay attention to what the experience of pain and trauma is telling you about what you truly value in your life and to imagine what shape those values might take with respect to your job and career, your health, your family relationships, and to all the other domains of your life affected by mobbing. A better future after mobbing is possible, and you can help that future along by taking seriously the hopeful stirrings of new possibilities that reflection and dialogue have offered.

For example, let's assume you were pushed out of your job at the end of a protracted period of mobbing. Concerning your career, what are the new possibilities to which you find yourself attracted? Do you want to stay in the same field or shift to a related field or are you interested in moving into an entirely new field? Is retiring an appealing and realistic possibility for you? Do your career interests allow for independent work or do you want to work within an organization again? What in the culture of a new organization would attract you and what would repel you? Do you want or need additional training or education? Do you need to make the same or more money than you did in the past or is making less money an option if you are doing satisfying work? How much of your daily and weekly life do you want to commit to work? What do your responses to these questions say about how you want your future work life to be and what do they tell you about work-related values and priorities that you may have overlooked or neglected in the past?

Shaping and formatting new possibilities for your future in the areas of your life most impacted by mobbing does not, needless to say, guarantee that these possibilities will all happen. However, envisioning a desirable future helps you to know more specifically what it is that you do want to happen and points you in the direction of steps that you can take in an effort to translate your vision of a better future into reality. Working on getting your life back after mobbing also involves attending to values and priorities that you may have disregarded prior to being mobbed. Paying attention to what is most meaningful and valuable to you in the areas impacted by mobbing can help you to get back a richer and more fulfilling life. You will have a different life after mobbing, but it does not have to be a diminished life. For example, those who have written about mobbing and bullying have noted that victims can become agents of change by sharing their stories of what happened and its impact.[20]

In addition to reflection, dialogue, and responding to the stirrings of new possibilities, getting your life back after mobbing also requires action on your part. Another way of thinking about taking action in the aftermath of mobbing is to think of it as your preferred way of responding to the effects of the trauma of workplace mobbing in your life. You have already mapped those effects in your life. Taking action empowers you to respond to those effects.[10,11,12]

The final step in using Tool #3, "How Do I Get My Life Back after Mobbing? Imagining Preferred Scenarios," involves taking some steps every day to enlarge the new possibilities you have identified for your life in order to help make these possibilities come alive. Every day take small steps to help transform your vision of a better future into reality. For example, if you identified the need to

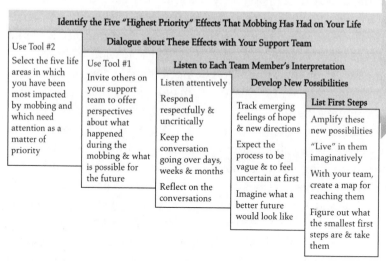

FIGURE 8.3 Tool #3: How Do I Get My Life Back after Mobbing?

improve your physical and psychological health after mobbing as "high priority" and you have a sense of what that improved health would look like, the final step in getting there is taking action. Do you need to eat better? To exercise regularly a few times a week? To get seven or eight hours of sleep per night? Are you accessing outside resources like psychotherapists or spiritual advisers or do you need to bring those kinds of resources on board? Are there other activities you can do to improve your health, like spending more time relaxing with your friends or family? Reading? Watching television? Taking up a new hobby or interest? Together with your support team, you are the one best positioned to map out the actions that you need to take to promote healing and recovery from mobbing in each of the areas of your life damaged by it. Start small and be consistent. Positive change will follow, and so will healing and recovery from mobbing.

Tracking How Your Recovery Is Going

As in our previous book about mobbing, we have intentionally used the term *victim* to refer to survivors of workplace mobbing. We have used the term to underscore and emphasize the fact that targets of workplace mobbing suffer occupational injuries as a result of the abuse and ostracism to which they have been subjected. Becoming a victim is the result of injury and/or abuse. We do not subscribe to the belief that use of the term *victim* has anything to do with weakness or self-pity or a refusal to go on with life. On the contrary, the many workplace mobbing victims with whom we have had contact want nothing more than to find a way to heal from the trauma of workplace mobbing and to go on with their lives as productively as possible.

In this section we provide a tool for helping mobbing victims to track how their recovery is going and to assess whether the new directions they are trying out are leading them where they want to go. In our experience, a frequent unexpected outcome of recovery from workplace mobbing is the unwillingness of victims to consider new work opportunities that do not reflect their interests and passions. Likewise, it is our experience that many victims trying to reestablish themselves in new work situations are more than happy to sacrifice money for increased job satisfaction and psychological safety. In trying out new directions for their lives after the trauma of workplace mobbing, victims may discover that there are other values and principles, previously overlooked, that they now wish to give expression to in their lives.

Tool #4, "Are These New Directions Contributing to My Recovery from Mobbing? Trying Out New Solutions, Possibilities, and Futures," shown in Figure 8.4, offers an iterative process for looking at the concrete steps you have taken to try out new possibilities for your future, to assess whether those possibilities match your current hopes and dreams for yourself, and to envision where those steps will lead should you continue with them. The tool is a segmented cycle that breaks down the process of tracking how your recovery is going into three interconnected parts.

In the first part, reflect on the question, "What steps have I taken to try out new possibilities for myself, family, and career?" Then list each step or new direction that you have tried and describe what the experience was like for you. You can write down your experiences of trying out new steps or tell people on your mobbing recovery support team what it was like. Think of new steps as any actions directed toward realizing your hopes and dreams and new possibilities. Their size or scope is not important. What's important is that a specific action related to possible new directions is involved. For example, making a list of your priorities for work–life balance or meeting with a career coach are both examples of taking steps in new directions. Invite the feedback of members of your support team who knew about or witnessed you trying out these new directions.

Next, think carefully about the question, "How has my vision of what I want for myself, family, and career changed since taking these steps in a new direction?" Fill in as much detail as you can about how your vision for yourself, your family, and your career has changed or evolved since you were mobbed. How is what you hope for in your work life, in your relationships with your family and friends, and in the way that you think about yourself different from before you were mobbed? What has become more important to you in your life and what has become less important? Acknowledging and honoring how you have changed since being mobbed is an important part of the process of healing and recovery.

The final step in using the tool involves thinking through where the new steps you have taken in your life toward recovery might lead if you continue with them. The question for reflection is, "If I keep on going with these steps in new directions, where will they lead for me, my family, and my career?" Do you like where these steps seem to be taking you and how you are feeling about these new directions? Are there any changes or revisions in your new direction that you think you need or want to make now? Do you have the sense that this new direction will lead to a good outcome for you and your family? This is the time to pay attention to how you feel about your possible new direction.

For example, a middle-aged man who was terminated in a workplace mobbing began to look for a job in an advertising agency after a couple of years of freelancing, at which he was only moderately successful. With the help of a business contact, he made it to the interview stage at a prestigious agency and was one of the final three candidates. After his second interview, he described feeling gloomy and like everything was closing in on him. He looked around his garden that had given him so much comfort and concluded that he wouldn't be able to care for it if he took the job. He realized that even before he got a job offer and knew anything about the reimbursement package he was starting to grieve for what he would be leaving behind. He talked with his wife and therapist and decided that it wasn't just fear—he didn't want the job and he didn't want to continue looking for work at advertising agencies. As a result of

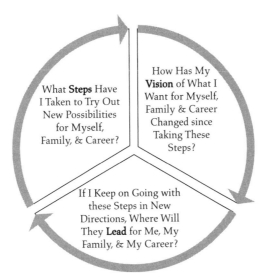

FIGURE 8.4 Tool #4: Are These New Directions Contributing to My Recovery from Mobbing?

trying out new directions in looking for work in an ad agency again, he decided against that option, and recommitted himself to developing his freelance work opportunities. You may like the new direction and how it feels or you may end up realizing that the new direction is not for you.

Conclusion

Our approach to recovery from mobbing relies on opposing the isolation foisted on a victim by making connections with carefully selected others and enjoying and utilizing those connections for companionship and support, as desired. Our approach also includes actively assessing the impact of mobbing on each of the domains of life impacted by it and understanding the meaning of the trauma of workplace mobbing for each person affected by it. Rather than moving away from the emotional and cognitive effects of mobbing, our approach involves moving closer to those effects so that they can be acknowledged and understood as fully as possible. Our approach to recovery from workplace mobbing recognizes that the story of the pain and suffering of the victim and victim's family is equally a story of their principles and beliefs about how to act in the world and how to treat others. Acknowledging the pain suffered by those who have been mobbed also acknowledges their values and beliefs, whether newly acquired or long-standing, about how work should be conducted, workers treated, and conflicts resolved. Our approach to recovery counters the hopelessness of mobbing with the development of new possibilities for one's life that are nurtured into shape by the everyday practices of recovery and healing. To facilitate these everyday practices of recovery, we have provided easy-to-use tools that bring the activities of healing and recovery into clearer focus.

The Healthy Workplace

W E BEGIN THIS CHAPTER WITH A BOLD STATEMENT: Healthy workplaces are respectful and accountable organizations that do *not* tolerate mobbing or any other form of interpersonal abuse or harassment. Surprisingly, such healthy and accountable organizations are often quite successful and productive; and, if they are in the private sector, they can be quite profitable. We add this qualifier because there is a common perception that during competitive and economically stressed times successful organizations often have to do "whatever it takes" to remain productive and profitable, including assigning the well-being of their employees a low priority.

In this chapter you will be introduced to the notion of organizational "health status" and the characteristics and markers of healthy-respectful and accountable organizations in contrast to mobbing-prone organizations. Examples of both will highlight the stark differences in health and accountability status between such organizations. The best personal strategy to safeguard against workplace mobbing is to seek out and work for a healthy-respectful organization. Therefore, the last part of this chapter includes an inventory that you can use to assess the health and accountability status of the place in which you work, or a place where you might consider working.

Organizational Health Status

Just as individuals can be characterized by their health status, so can organizations. Individual health status refers to the overall well-being, fitness, and disease processes or injuries for a specific individual. Organizational health status refers to the organization's overall performance *and* the health and well-being of its employees.[1] There are two dimensions in organizational health status. The first is overall organization performance, which can be assessed in terms of productivity (and profitability) as well as in terms of accountability. The second dimension is overall employee health and well-being, which can be assessed in terms of job satisfaction, morale, loyalty and commitment to the organization, and personal physical and emotional well-being. Organizations can be high or low in one or both dimensions.

The healthiest organizations are high in both dimensions. As a general rule, organizations in which mobbing is fostered *and* occurs are those low in the employee health and well-being dimension; and, while such organizations can be high or low on the performance dimension, they tend to be low in accountability. We will refer to organizations that foster mobbing as mobbing-prone organizations, and organizations that discourage mobbing and foster respect as mobbing-resistant/healthy-respectful organizations. Instead of being polar opposites, organizations can be best represented on a continuum in which the end points are mobbing-prone and mobbing-resistant— also known as healthy-respectful—organizations.

Placing organizations on such a continuum reflects the reality of organizational life, which is to say that some organizations that have fostered mobbing in the past no longer do so because of intentional organizational change. Similarly, other organizations with no history of mobbing have later experienced it for any number of reasons. Figure 9.1 visualizes this continuum.

Mobbing-Prone   Mobbing-Resistant

FIGURE 9.1 Organizational Continuum: From Mobbing-Prone to Mobbing-Resistant.

Accountability and Health Status

At the beginning of this chapter we said that healthy workplaces—those with high health status—are respectful and accountable organizations and that they do *not* tolerate mobbing. They are the opposite of mobbing-prone organizations. Short of workplace mobbing being reported in the news, how can one determine the health status of a particular organization? Here we'll describe how organizations typically portray themselves in terms of their mission, vision, and values. We'll also describe organizational accountability, a very useful marker of health status.

One place to start is the organization's portrayal of itself in its mission, vision, and values statements. This portrayal, or aspects of it, is usually described in the organization's annual report, employee handbook, marketing material, press releases, and on organization websites. For example, connected to an organization's mission statement is its values statement, which is often more useful and important for a consumer to read and understand than the mission statement. The values statement can be particularly helpful in understanding what the organization is really about, because it describes what the organization says it values most. A common theme runs through most of the value statements that we have studied from both for-profit and not-for-profit organizations, whether they are Fortune 500 corporations or small family businesses. Typically, this common theme is a focus on customer orientation and on the organization's products or services. Some values statements even briefly mention employees, providing a deeper look into the organization itself. These published statements offer clues to the organizations' values and their priorities. They help potential customers and employees know what the organization values and how it operationalizes these values and priorities. They also offer some help to current and potential employees in evaluating how their personal values match the organization's values, as well as in understanding what might be expected of them.

Let's consider the topic of accountability and what useful criteria for holding an organization accountable are. It is critical to know *to whom* and *for what* an organization is accountable. It is vital to identify "to whom" and "for what" an organization is *actually* accountable irrespective of what its *stated* accountability is. For example, some organizations are only accountable to their shareholders and boards of directors (for-profits) or to their boards of directors alone (not-for-profits). Conversely, other organizations demonstrate by their actions that they are accountable to a range of stakeholders, including customers, employees, the wider community, and so on. The broader the range of actual "to whoms" organizations are accountable, the less likely they are to be mobbing-prone. Likewise, the more "for whats" an organization is accountable, the less likely they are to be mobbing-prone. These "for whats" are manifest in the *actual* core values.

Whether an organization does, in fact, operationalize its actual values and priorities so that its real-world behaviors match its stated values and priorities can be either a source of organizational pride or a source of organizational confusion. If stated and actual values do match, the values statement can motivate and guide employees in their work as well as create a sense of loyalty and satisfaction for them in being part of that organization. When there is a mismatch or disconnect between stated and actual values, employees tend to respond in kind by manifesting disloyalty to the organization.

The extent to which organizations are accountable and succeed with certain priorities and values is of considerable interest to the business community. Every year, magazines like *Fortune* and other rating services publish lists of the "best companies." These include "The 100 Best Companies to Work For," "The World's Most Admired Companies," "The 100 Most Family-Friendly Companies," and "The World's Most Ethical Companies." The Malcolm Baldrige National Quality Award recognizes organizations with high organizational health status both in terms of measures of corporate performance and in terms of workforce engagement and well-being. There are various routes that companies can take to achieve recognition on one of the lists of best companies and to be considered for the Malcolm Baldrige National Quality Award.

The Baldrige Award and some of the lists of best companies require that candidate companies submit detailed applications about their organizations. Some lists require that a company be nominated or nominate itself. Still other lists are developed from the opinions and perspectives obtained by surveys of industry leaders and insiders. Whatever the methodology, getting listed on one of the best companies' lists or winning a Baldrige Award for quality management is highly desirable and is based on a fairly substantial amount of company data. Such ratings can provide a useful window into an organization. Some highly profitable organizations regularly make the "Fortune 500," a list of the 500 largest companies in the United States by gross revenue, but seldom if ever appear on other lists associated with excellence in employee well-being and ethical practices. For those companies that never apply or are not selected for the lists showcasing employee well-being and ethical practices, absence from these lists can be suggestive of a greater focus on performance and productivity than on employee health and well-being.

In contrast, there are some organizations that are consistently recognized for both performance and health. For example, in 2012 Google was ranked 73rd in the Fortune 500 and was also ranked as the number-one large company to work for by *Fortune*. As well as being profitable and innovative, Google is consistently ranked as one of the best companies to work for in *Fortune*'s rankings and by the *Human Rights Campaign* as one of the "Best Places to Work for LGBT Equality." Google regularly wins other important recognition such as being listed in *Fortune* magazine's "World's Most Admired Companies," *Forbes* magazine's "America's Most Reputable Company," and *Fortune* magazine's "100 Best Companies to Work For."[2] Similarly, Starbucks is listed in three key health-performance categories: *Fortune* magazine's "World's Most Admired Companies," in its "100 Best Companies to Work For," and in the *Ethisphere Institute's* "World's Most Ethical Companies" for every year the award has been given.[3]

What is the reason for these high ratings? Most likely, the answer is Google's and Starbucks' high overall health status. In other words, such organizations are able both to be profitable and to promote the health and well-being of employees. Such organizations operationalize their core values and priorities and have histories of being accountable and responsible for their actions. This is in marked contrast to organizations that are mobbing-prone and demonstrate less accountability and responsibility for their actions, that instead resort to excuses, blame, and even threats. This low level of accountability is illustrated in the second case study later in this chapter.

Organizational Types and Health Status

Let's take a brief look at the types of organizations—and some indicators of organizational health status—in which workplace mobbing is likely to occur. Three distinct organizational types and their views about mobbing are described by Patricia Ferris, an organizational psychologist and consultant.[4] In the first type, mobbing is viewed as acceptable behavior. In the second type, mobbing is viewed as simply a personality conflict, while in the third type, it is viewed as harmful and inappropriate. She colloquially refers to these organizational types as "see no evil," "hear no evil," and "speak no evil." We have found this typology quite useful in understanding the distinctive ways in which organizations characteristically respond to mobbing. Here is a brief description.

Type 1: See No Evil

This type of organization emphasizes both productivity and profits and is accountable primarily toward shareholders rather than employees. Not surprisingly, employees in such organizations experience high levels of work stress and considerable pressure to achieve and meet tight deadlines. Such organizations are characterized by high job strain, meaning that while employees are faced with high demands for job performance they perceive themselves as having little to no control over the manner in which they perform their jobs. Turnover is high, morale tends to be low, and benefit use for medical care and psychiatric services is high.

Managers, including human resources (HR) managers, tend to be defensive about mobbing. They may even be willing to admit that such negative behavior is considered acceptable in their organization. But, they tend to attribute the cause of mobbing to "weakness" or "problematic behavior" on the part of the targeted employee and are likely to be dismissive of complaints of mobbing. When managers in "see no evil" organizations intervene, their actions typically consist of advising the targeted employee to toughen up and increase his or her resilience. Employees in such organizations characteristically report high overall stress levels, high-to-excessive work volume, and significant pressure to perform. They are not surprised that HR is unhelpful and dismissive of concerns about mobbing behaviors and workplace abuse, in general. Often, they are aware of their organization's lack of focus on employee health and well-being and have witnessed many injustices within the organization. Not surprisingly, targeted employees tend to quit rather than request assistance from the organization.

Their "see no evil" view is evident in the conscious choices these organizations make regarding mobbing. They see mobbing as normal and acceptable behavior. Occasionally, they may acknowledge harm to the employee but see it as representing weakness on the part of the employee and subsequently advise the target-victim to toughen up and become less reactive to the abusive behaviors. The culture of these organizations is achievement oriented, focused primarily on profit, with accountability focused toward shareholders and their board of directors.

Type 2: Hear No Evil

These organizations are often, but not always, educational, health care, or governmental institutions. Employees may serve in professional job classifications with job expectations and reporting relationships that are usually clearly specified. The culture of these organizations is often rule-oriented and bureaucratic. Often they have respectful workplace policies and codes of conduct. These policies and codes seldom include provisions about mobbing since employees are not protected from it by federal statute as they are from sexual harassment and racial discrimination. Nonetheless, employees expect that their organization will implement policies and codes against mobbing and other types of workplace abuse and are surprised or shocked to learn that either such codes and policies do not exist or, if they exist, are inconsistently enforced. Management in such organizations is hierarchical, and accountability is primarily directed toward meeting annual indices as well as statutory or accreditation standards, with concern for the well-being of employees remaining secondary.

This "hear no evil" view is evident in managers' representation of mobbing as merely a "personality conflict" between two or more employees. The last thing such managers want to hear is that an employee is being targeted by other employees. Instead, both parties are assumed to be responsible for the conflict. The targeted employee may even be blamed for having the type of personality that aggravates or provokes the perpetrators. When managers intervene it is to tell the parties involved to solve the problem themselves. Another common reaction is to deny that the situation is an "organization problem" because the aggressive behaviors cannot be classified as targeted against members of protected groups based on race, religion, age, gender, sexual orientation, and so on.

Managers who wash their hands when confronted with reports of aggressive workplace behaviors suffer from a basic misunderstanding of the dynamics of mobbing. In these kinds of "hear no evil" organizations, mediation is often available to resolve conflicts. But such a strategy of focusing only on the individuals involved will not result in the needed changes to organizational dynamics. When mediation fails or is counter-productive, as is often the case in mobbing situations, extensive counseling may be required to help victimized employees cope with the lack of help or the failed mediation.

When victimized employees conclude that their organization is unlikely to actively support them, legal action is considered. Because of the extent to which victimized employees in such "hear no evil" organizations were negatively impacted by mobbing, these employees were found to require more therapy than similarly victimized employees from the other two types of organizations. The "hear no evil" type of organizations may be most damaging to employees because they foster the belief that they value respectful workplaces while not backing up their stated values with effective action plans to implement them. In these kinds of organizations, employees expect that the organization will intervene in ongoing mobbing and other forms of workplace aggression by implementing nonharassment measures and reinstating a respectful workplace. When such an organizational response is not forthcoming, employees typically feel betrayed and may pursue legal action once they understand that they are unlikely to receive active support from their organization.

Type 3: Speak No Evil

Most often, "speak no evil" types of organizations are for-profit organizations that have taken action against mobbing at some time in the past and have mismanaged it. Following their ineffective actions, management has made purposeful changes to the organization's culture, structure, and leadership, resulting in the proactive development of a more mobbing-resistant organization in which the culture is characterized by respect and in which management style reflects support for employees. In addition, management revised the organization's nonharassment policies to include mobbing, required nonharassment training for managers, and provided coaching and counseling to employees who have been victims of workplace abuse, while investigating and making every effort to resolve the abusive situation.

The "speak no evil" view is evident in this type of organization's clear acknowledgment that mobbing is inappropriate and harmful. Since gossip and defamation act as both kindling and fuel for mobbing, the management in speak-no-evil types of organizations understands that an uptick in such verbal abuse is a red flag requiring attention and possibly intervention. The organization's commitment to a mobbing-free workplace is also reflected in management's strategies to maintain a respectful and safe workplace for everyone, in their policies and procedures that include effective antimobbing policies that do more than offer lip service, and in their implementation of antimobbing awareness and training initiatives for supervisors and employees. Additionally, comprehensive coaching, counseling, and performance management strategies have been designed to effectively address issues involving workplace mobbing and related abuse.

In sum, the first two types represent mobbing-prone organizations, while the third reflects a healthier, more respectful organization. The next two sections illustrate organizations with very different health statuses. The first describes a healthy organization that has never experienced reports of mobbing, while the second describes an organization that fosters mobbing.

Example of a Healthy, Mobbing-Resistant Workplace

Catholic Health Services (CHS) is the largest not-for-profit comprehensive post-acute health care system in the southeastern United States. It has four medical campuses in South Florida that include acute medical rehabilitation hospitals, specialty outpatient clinics, home health services, hospice care, long-term care and skilled nursing facilities—also called nursing homes—as well as assisted living. They also offer low-income housing for independent seniors and other community services. Over the past three decades thousands of people have recovered greater independence, improved their health, or have found comfort through utilizing their services.[5]

Mission, Vision, and Values

The stated *mission statement* of CHS is "to provide health care and services to those in need, to minimize human suffering, to assist people to wholeness, and to nurture an awareness of their relationship with God." The stated *vision statement* of CHS is "to strive to improve the health, independence, and spiritual life of the elderly, the poor, and the needy, through innovative and proactive approaches to managing care and providing services; facilitating transitions across levels of care; community partnerships and collaboration; and advocacy efforts." Their *values statement* indicates that their first priority is their patients, the second is their employees, and third is their community.[5]

CHS Values Statement

"We believe our first responsibility is to our patients, residents, our families and all others who use our services....Our second responsibility is to our employees, the men and women who enable us to care for our patients and clients. We will respect our employees' dignity, recognize their merit and value their contributions to Catholic Health Services. We will provide the resources to uphold their dedication to excellence. Our third responsibility is to our community. We understand that our responsibility extends beyond the physical walls of our building and into our communities. We will serve to the best of our financial ability—those unable to afford. Our final responsibility is to the future. We will be faithful stewards of our resources to preserve our ability to carry out our Mission and serve our communities for generations to come."[5]

The stated *core values* of CHS are dignity, commitment, excellence, and stewardship. Dignity means that patients, families, and employees are accorded respect regardless of race, creed, or religious affiliation and economic status. Commitment is a firm decision to focus energy on the successful completion of goals in the spirit of a specific mission. Excellence is a dedication to establishing and meeting high personal, spiritual, professional, and organizational goals and standards. Stewardship is the good use of organizational resources, both human and material.[5]

Patient Satisfaction

Patient satisfaction measures patients' opinions of the quality of customer service provided to them and to their family members and visitors during their hospital stay. CHS uses a patient satisfaction system that is uniquely designed to provide immediate feedback to CHS management and employees. Within 24 hours of receiving a low rating on any item on the survey from patient and family—ranging from concerns about food to nursing care—the family is called to learn how the matter might be resolved. Simultaneously, management contacts supervisors of the unit caring for the patient so that they can work to rectify the concern through collaboration with appropriate employees and the patient and patient's family. This immediate attention to its patients-customers reflects CHS's intentional effort to live up to its values statement: "Our first responsibility is to our patients, residents, our families." What is particularly impressive is that current and prospective patients and their families have direct access to recent patient satisfaction scores. A tab on the CHS website allows easy access to the "Realtime Patient Satisfaction Survey Report" results for all of its medical facilities.[6] Few health care facilities have this much transparency. For us, this level of transparency is a key indicator of how CHS demonstrates its core values of dignity, commitment, excellence, and stewardship.

Values Audit

Values audits are utilized by organizations wanting to evaluate the match between stated core values and the actual or practiced core values of their organization. The premise is that the closer the match between stated and actual core values, the higher the levels of employee job satisfaction, commitment, morale, and productivity. We are impressed that CHS is committed to this audit and uses an outside consulting firm to ensure the validity of the results. The results of a recent audit revealed that there was a high degree of match on nearly all of the items in the survey, and a subsequent effort to increase the degree of match on one item. Overall, this values audit was consistent with its low employee turnover rate, high productivity, and high levels of employee satisfaction, morale, and commitment. It also demonstrated that CHS works hard to live up to its values statement: "Our second responsibility is to our employees."

Community Impact

CHS has both local and national impact. CHS provides over $10 million in local community benefit services each year. Their nationally recognized programs range from health education and free screenings to clinical and ancillary medical services training to doctoral-level internships in rehabilitation hospitals. Community partnerships vary from affiliation with local universities, colleges, and high schools to advocacy groups for awareness, campaigns, screenings, workshops, and support groups. Recently, CHS was chosen by the Centers for Medicare and Medicaid Services to be 1 of 17 national demonstration sites on evaluating quality assurance and performance. Carol Preston, CHS director of quality control, said: "It's a great chance for us to help in nationwide decision making affecting nursing homes and build on our existing Quality Improvement efforts."[7] These contributions and efforts demonstrate how CHS lives up to its values statement: "Our third responsibility is to our community."

Reflections about a Mobbing-Resistant Organization

CHS represents the healthy, mobbing-resistant end point on the organizational continuum (Figure 9.1). In many ways CHS seems too good to be true. One of its rehabilitation hospitals is consistently rated the best in the country, it has the lowest turnover rate of any hospital in the region, most employees retire with 30 or more years of service, patient satisfaction is near 97%, and mobbing has never been reported there. In contrast to most of its peers it is also profitable. In short, CHS has a very high health status.

Example of a Mobbing-Prone Workplace

Florida A&M University (FAMU) has been in the national news since the hazing-related death of FAMU drum major Robert Champion.

The university student was beaten to death during a hazing ritual that occurred aboard a charter bus returning from a football game. Prior to Champion's death band members reportedly were challenging the newly promoted drum major's authority.[8] Twelve band members were charged with felonies and two with misdemeanor hazing that resulted in Champion's death. The beatings exposed a "violent culture in the band that had festered for years,"[8] which ultimately led to the resignation of the university president and others in positions of authority.

Hazing is a centuries-old ritual of initiation for fraternal organizations like fraternities, sororities, and invitation-only groups like clubs and sports teams. In the past, universities and other fraternal organizations have tacitly permitted hazing, presuming it to be a harmless ritual. However, hazing can be disabling and even deadly. In an effort to maintain student safety and reduce exposure to liability, nearly all colleges and universities have initiated antihazing policies. Unfortunately, such policies are not always enforced.

The National Study of Student Hazing surveys more than 11,000 undergraduates at 53 universities. Hazing is defined as "any activity expected of someone joining or participating in a group that humiliates, degrades, abuses, or endangers them regardless of a person's willingness to participate."[9] Humiliation, paddling, sexual acts, isolation, sleep-deprivation, and alcohol consumption were identified in the study as common hazing practices. Over 55% of students involved in university organizations reported being hazed. However, 74% of those involved in varsity sports teams, sororities, and fraternities experienced some hazing behaviors. Surprisingly, 25% of coaches or organization advisers were aware of their groups' hazing behaviors, and the clear implication is that they did nothing to stop them.[9] Since these coaches and advisers were in leadership positions and represented their universities, hazing meets the criteria for mobbing and not simply bullying. In short, hazing is a form of mobbing when the organization colludes with those carrying out hazing rituals by remaining silent and doing little or nothing to stop the hazing. Such is the case of FAMU.

The *Sun Sentinel* newspaper chronicled Champion's hazing experience and death from the first report about the incident through the extended legal aftermath. It reported that the FAMU legal defense team submitted a motion to dismiss the wrongful death lawsuit filed by Champion's parents. The motion contained the following statement: "Respectfully as a 26 year old adult and leader in FAMU's band, Mr. Champion should have refused to participate in the planned hazing event and report it to law enforcement or university administrators. Under these circumstances, Florida's taxpayers should not be held financially liable to Mr. Champion's estate for the ultimate result of his own imprudent, avoidable and tragic decision and death."[10]

Later, the university deleted this statement from the motion, but continued to blame Champion in a kinder, gentler manner. Instead of working with his family on a resolution, FAMU continued to utilize the "blame the victim" strategy so familiar in mobbing. Nevertheless, the motion continued to maintain that Champion had signed the school's antihazing policy and that he knew that hazing violated state law and university policy. Furthermore, they claimed that Champion was 26 years old, was the band's drum major, and as an adult should have known better than to subject himself to hazing.

In the course of the investigation it was reported that the FAMU president and band director were forced to resign because of their inaction in containing hazing. Also noted was a long history of hazing-related injuries and legal actions involving the marching band. The newspaper reported that the school "ignored a dean's call in November to bench the band before Champion's death to curb hazing."[11]

While many organizations and universities tout their stated core value of "customers (or students) come first," the actions of mobbing-prone organizations like FAMU suggest that their actual core values may be "students come last." That the culture of FAMU is mobbing-prone is noted in a *Sun Sentinel* editorial on September 18, 2012: The university "publicly and defiantly abdicates responsibility for student safety, tacitly endorsing a culture where ritualistic beatings are part of fitting in."[11]

Reflections about a Mobbing-Prone Organization

FAMU is mobbing-prone and represents a "See No Evil" organization. It has failed in its accountability to its stakeholders. The case of Robert Champion illustrates its strategy of blaming the victim— a dead victim—and his family. The FAMU story has increased antihazing sentiment to the point that some are proposing that federal financial aid be denied students who are punished by universities for hazing or convicted of it. Since hazing is a form of mobbing because of the organization's involvement in it by turning a blind eye, such proposals to punish only students miss the point. It would be more fitting and more effective for both the university as well as the involved students to be sanctioned.

Conclusion

Healthy organizations are respectful and accountable workplaces that are mobbing-resistant. Traditionally, organizations were evaluated primarily in terms of their profitability and productivity. If they were making money they were doing well, and if they weren't making money they were doing poorly. In this old-school view, organizational health and vitality were measured in terms of performance alone. Today, organizational reputation is increasingly important, and many organizations, both large and small, spend a lot of time and effort investing in strategies that promote employee health and well-being and workforce engagement.

Companies want to be recognized not just as good but as great places to work and make the many different lists of "best companies to work for." Combining the traditional dimension of performance and profitability with the employee health and well-being dimension provides the fullest and best picture of organizational health. Companies and organizations that score high on both dimensions are the healthiest, the most mobbing-resistant, and most likely to be really good places to work. A new kind of workers' rights movement is beginning to emerge. The focus has shifted to call attention to employee concerns that workplaces are respectful, fair, and proactive in preventing mobbing and other forms of workplace abuse. The shape of this movement is visible. If you haven't felt its power yet, you soon will.

To get a sense of the overall health status of your own workplace or a place where you are considering working you can do a little research and fill out the checklists below. A small investment of time and effort can help you protect your own health and well-being by checking out the health status of your workplace.

Assessing the Health Status of Your Workplace

Directions: You can use the following checklists to assess the health status of your current or prospective workplace. Before completing the checklists, do the best you can to collect information about the workplace; for example, research stated versus actual core values, employee turnover rates, decisional control, customer and employee satisfaction surveys, and so on by reviewing websites or documents and by talking to current or former employees. There are 10 items on each checklist. The more items that you check on the list, the more the workplace resembles either a mobbing-resistant or mobbing-prone organization.

A mobbing-resistant/healthy-respectful workplace:

____ practices what it preaches; its stated core values match its actual core values

____ is accountable and responsible for its actions without excuses, blame, or threats

____ respects employees, and employees reciprocate with loyalty

____ tends to have low turnover as well as high morale and job satisfaction

____ fosters decisional control over how workers do their jobs, take breaks, vacations, and so on

____ is family-friendly

____ tends to be "a good neighbor" and supports its surrounding community

____ is or could be on a list of "best places to work"

____ fosters the health and well-being of employees

____ tends to be productive and profitable while maintaining high ethical standards

A mobbing-prone workplace:

____ seldom practices what it preaches; there is a disconnect between stated and actual values

____ is not accountable or responsible for its actions and resorts to excuses, blame, or threats

____ tends to disrespect employees, and employees reciprocate with disloyalty

____ tends to have high turnover as well as low morale and job satisfaction

____ does not foster decisional control by workers over their job, breaks, vacations, and so on

____ is not family-friendly

____ is neither a "good neighbor" nor supportive of the surrounding community

____ is not likely to be on a list of "best places to work"

____ fosters illness and disability over the well-being of employees

____ tends to emphasize productivity and profitability but at the expense of ethical standards

Toward a Better, Mobbing-Free Future

T O THINK ABOUT THE PROBLEM OF WORKPLACE mobbing requires acknowledging that everything is not right within our workplaces and organizations. Too many people work in organizations where they are at risk for mobbing and other forms of workplace abuse and where the organizational culture is psychologically unsafe for them. This is a discouraging acknowledgment especially in a time when jobs are relatively scarce and the ethos of the times is "just be happy that you have a job, don't complain, and suck up whatever is going on that you don't like." Ignoring problems doesn't make them go away, of course, and in this book we have taken a hard look at the vexing problem of workplace mobbing. Margaret Heffernan, the author of a recent business best seller, *Willful Blindness: Why We Ignore the Obvious at Our Peril*, reminds us that it takes courage to see and to name what is right in front of us and that, in most instances, refusing to see leads us down ever more slippery slopes and dangerous paths. She writes, "We may think being blind makes us safer, when in fact it leaves us crippled, vulnerable, and powerless. But when we confront facts and fears, we achieve real power and unleash our capacity for change."[1] Denying or minimizing the existence and effects of workplace mobbing is not helpful to anyone.

The point of examining workplace mobbing is to shed more light on it by explaining what it is, what it looks and feels like, what causes it, and what effects it has on its victims and on the organizations in which they work. The larger point, of course, is to take the results of this analysis of workplace mobbing and to extrapolate some realistic, practical, and effective takeaways that will allow us to prevent it and to heal the damage inflicted by it, without causing unintended negative consequences in the process.

Almost all of us work for a significant part of our lives. Consequently, we have a shared interest in creating mobbing-resistant, humane, and psychologically safe organizations within which to work. So, as we conclude this book, let's do so by trying to tease out of our analysis of workplace mobbing some key takeaways for making organizations and the communication and behavior within them safer and more mobbing-resistant for everyone. These key takeaways, as with the rest of our book, challenge long-standing mythology about the "bad apple" or "rotten egg" explanations for workplace mobbing. They also represent reminders of what to do in order to advance our shared interest of crafting more humane and healthy workplaces.

Takeaway #1: Most People Who Display Aggressive, Mobbing-Type Behaviors in the Workplace Are "Normal"

The prevalence of people with antisocial personality disorder, the type associated with blatant disregard of the rights and feelings of others and a corresponding willingness to violate other peoples' rights in order to get what they want, is low. In samples of the general community, about 1% of females and 3% of males are believed to have antisocial personality disorder.[2] What these prevalence figures mean for workplace mobbing and aggression is that most of those who participate in aggressive workplace behaviors do not meet the criteria for the mental illnesses or personality disorders most associated with the kinds of behaviors that are typical in workplace mobbing. These figures just corroborate our position that it is the interaction of complex individual, group, and organizational behavior that results in mobbing—not individuals who fall outside of the range of so-called normal behavior.

Takeaway #2: Given the Right Constellation of Individual, Group, and Organizational Influences, Many If Not Most People Could End up Participating in Ganging up and Workplace Mobbing

This is a sobering if not shocking thought. Group pressure, a part of the process of workplace mobbing, is likely to result in increased personal disinhibition or lowering of restraints that would otherwise be in place for individuals in the absence of group pressure. Disinhibition in the context of group pressure increases the likelihood that individuals will behave in ways that they would ordinarily not. Combining the disinhibition associated with group pressure with an absence of reflection about the meaning and effects of one's behavior on others creates a potent cocktail in which otherwise good people are more likely to act in ways that hurt others.

Hannah Arendt, the famous philosopher and political theorist who studied evil in the context of Nazism, wrote that "the sad truth of the matter is that most evil is done by people who never made up their minds to be or do either evil or good."[3] In other words, they never bothered to think about the meaning and implications of their actions for others. Arendt coined the well-known phrase the "banality of evil"[4] to highlight the absence of reflection and interior dialogue that she believed was associated with the emergence of evil. Extending Arendt's ideas to workplaces suggests that mobbing and other abuse happen in work contexts marked by the absence of thinking about and making space for the other. An attitude of compassion, a willingness to put oneself in another's shoes, and meaningful concern for the well-being of others in the organization are the kinds of behaviors that create psychologically safe workplaces. What's more, these attitudes and behaviors are not inconsistent with profitability, as we discussed in the previous chapter. By comparison, humiliation and the failure of empathy are tools of violence and are routinely employed in workplace mobbings. Preventing humiliation in the workplace and increasing empathy would together go a long way toward reducing workplace mobbing and its destructive effects. The wisdom of Arendt's ideas also opens pathways for positive change by organizational members at any level. Past failures to consider the implications of one's behaviors on coworkers, supervisors, and super-visees need not govern present and future behavior.

Native American eco-spirituality requires thinking ahead and working on behalf of the seventh generation going forward. Much workplace mobbing and other workplace abuse could be reduced simply by thinking about the impact of decisions, communicative behaviors, and other workplace actions on the health and well-being of other employees in the workplace and on their families, whether one knows their families or not. Such a standard falls far short of the Native American seventh generation standard, but it does involve deliberate mindfulness of the impact of workplace behavior on other people and their families—a one circle outward standard. Considering "the other" in this way, by itself, would be a powerful antidote to an absence of reflection and, by extension, to workplace mobbing.

Takeaway #3: Psychosocial Health Risks, in Particular Workplace Mobbing, Are Not Included in Most Workplace Health and Well-Being Policies and Programs and Must Be in Order to Address Significant Sources of Harm and Risk to Individual, Family, and Organizational Health

As we described in chapter 9, employee health and well-being is a central focus of healthy organizations, and we have contended that psychosocial health risks, especially mobbing, must be clearly addressed in policy and program development in order to maximize employee health and address known current risks to health. We take this position because it is a sound business strategy for improving overall business performance and because it is the right thing to do. Mobbing is a widespread and increasing threat to worker health and is a recognized risk to both worker and organizational health.

The healthy workplace has been a focus for the World Health Organization (WHO), which regards healthy workplaces as a pri-mary site of health promotion and health protection for workers, their families, and their communities. WHO has proposed a defini-tion of a healthy workplace that is directed toward prevention, health protection, and avoidance of reinjury when a person returns to work following a health incident. We think it is worth stating WHO's definition of a healthy workplace here to emphasize that concern for worker health and safety, including worker psychosocial health and safety—for example, freedom from mobbing—has been recognized globally. Here is WHO's definition:

> A healthy workplace is one in which workers and managers collaborate to use a continual improvement process to protect and promote the health, safety and well-being of workers and the sustainability of the workplace by considering the following, based on identified needs:
>
> - health and safety concerns in the physical work environment;
> - health, safety and well-being concerns in the psychosocial work environment including organization of work and workplace culture;
> - personal health resources in the workplace; and
> - ways of participating in the community to improve the health of workers, their families and other members of the community.[5]

Understanding what is meant by psychological and psychosocial safety in the workplace is a rapidly evolving area of focus for policy and the law in most Western countries. Workplace mobbing is recognized as a current workplace health hazard and is therefore a central consideration where psychosocial health risks are concerned. The problem is that most corporate policy and programming, as of this writing, are silent on the issue. As regional and national standards for addressing psychosocial health and well-being of workers are developed and refined, we fully expect that workplace mobbing will increasingly be identified as a specific psychosocial workplace hazard that organizations have a responsibility to prevent.

Globally, the World Health Organization already recognizes mobbing as a psychosocial workplace stressor that organizations must prevent.[5] A 2009 Canadian report on workplace stress, mental injury, and the law[6] mapped out the new terrain that employers must now traverse as a result of evolving community standards holding them responsible for protection of the psychosocial and psychological health of workers. Findings from this report included:

- The protection of mental health at work can be seen both as a corporate and as a social responsibility, with legal implications in each case. At a corporate level, the primary implication of the legal developments revealed by this study are that the provision of a psychologically safe workplace is a governance and stewardship issue in the same way that the provision of a physically safe workplace is... .

- At a minimum, risks to employee mental health arising from the organization and design of work should be on every corporate risk register and a corresponding policy should be in place to abate such risks once discovered.[6]

In terms of psychosocial work hazards like mobbing, the future is clear. Organizations and employers are increasingly likely to be held accountable for how they manage known psychosocial hazards like mobbing. How employers treat employees, how employees treat each other, how employers manage unethical workplace communication, how employers manage vulnerable workers, how employers manage demotions and dismissals already are, and will increasingly become, contested sites where employees who have been psychologically harmed seek redress.

Takeaway #4: Anyone Who Has Ever Worked Has Made Mistakes. Mistakes, Whether at the Individual, Group, or Organizational Level, Are in and of Themselves Not the Biggest Problem. The Biggest Problem Is the Failure to Acknowledge and Repair the Mistakes

There will always be ruptures in human relationships—times when we are out of attunement and out of alignment with one another. In early attachment relationships, maintaining a sense of safety and security requires repair of relationship ruptures.[7,8] For adults, work is also critical to a sense of security and safety in the world, while consisting of very different relationships from those early attachment ones. Because work signifies making a living for most adults, threats to one's job and work as a result of workplace mobbing represent actual life threats[9] requiring urgent attention and repair if the victim is to avoid traumatic repercussions.

Repair is both possible and necessary once workplace mobbing or other abuse has been identified. It just takes courage to do it.

Repairing the rupture caused by workplace mobbing requires both acknowledgment of the wrongdoing and actions designed to help make the victim whole again. Let's take a look at the process of repair in the aftermath of workplace mobbing at the organizational, group, and individual levels.

Organization

You might first think that an organization cannot repair the damage done to a victim as a result of workplace mobbing because if the organization acknowledged wrongdoing it would be sued and made liable for a range of wrongs and harms done. While that may be true, it could happen whether the organization made an effort to engage in repair or not. Consider the research and reports about physicians who made mistakes resulting in injury to their patients, even serious and fatal injury, who then sincerely apologized to the patients and/ or their family members.[10,11,12] The physicians who apologized were sued less often than their counterparts who did not apologize. On top of that, the patients and family members involved felt better because they were given the complete picture of what happened and were not left in the dark, guessing, trying to piece together what happened by themselves.

Charles Duhigg's book *The Power of Habit: Why We Do What We Do in Life and Business*[13] includes a story about Paul O'Neill, the former chairman and CEO of Alcoa and former secretary of the treasury under President George W. Bush. The story leaves most who read it with chills. O'Neill went to Alcoa with the express intention of making worker safety a non-negotiable top priority—whatever it took and whatever it cost. Six months into his tenure, O'Neill was told that a recent hire in an Arizona plant had been killed trying to make a repair on a piece of malfunctioning equipment. The worker had jumped over a yellow safety wall to get to the equipment to try and fix it, which he did, but was hit in the head by the swinging arm of the machine as it restarted.

At an emergency meeting of Alcoa's top executives from the local plant and headquarters, called within 14 hours of the worker's death, O'Neill is quoted as saying: "We killed this man. It's my failure of leadership. I caused his death. And it's the failure of all of you in the chain of command."[13] This is an example of no-holds-barred acceptance of corporate responsibility even though the company had a massive worker safety program under way and even though the worker who was killed had crossed a yellow safety wall to get to the equipment, facts that would presumably have mitigated the degree of corporate responsibility in the case. O'Neill's stunning acceptance of corporate responsibility for the tragedy also powerfully made the point that his company was better than that, his organization and people could do better than that, and he was making no excuses. O'Neill's behavior illustrates what organizational nondefensiveness at its best can look like. We doubt that it is coincidental that, under O'Neill's leadership, Alcoa's stock price also rose 200% and that on measures of both performance and employee health and well-being, Alcoa was a stellar performer.

Just for a moment, let's return to the case of Robert Champion, the drum major who was beaten to death at FAMU in a hazing ritual, and consider the corporate response to that tragedy. The initial motion filed by FAMU's legal defense team in response to the wrongful death lawsuit filed by Champion's parents argued that Champion was a 26-year-old adult who should not have voluntarily participated in a known hazing event.[14] First of all, suggesting that a band member was free to not participate in the long-standing and widely known hazing rituals of the marching band, a campus institution, is not a lot different than saying that someone with a gun pointed at his or her head is free to leave the room. Instead of blaming the victim, how might things have been different for FAMU and for Robert Champion's family if the leadership at FAMU had taken a page from Paul O'Neill's book, accepted responsibility, and made a commitment that Champion's legacy at FAMU would be the elimination of hazing from that university and the assurance that no other student would ever be faced with the choice of having to "cross Bus C"?

Group(s)

Within groups, the greatest challenge to acknowledgment and repair of wrongdoing in workplace mobbing is recognizing and stopping the flow of unethical communication, and, once it has occurred, correcting its destructive effects. We have discussed unethical communication at length and illustrated how it provides fuel for workplace mobbing, especially through its dissemination among groups within the workplace.

For example, in a study of workplace mobbing in Turkish universities a hostile faction of faculty members ganged up to mob another faculty member.[15] This group of faculty members recruited students to join in the mob against the target faculty member. Their primary method of persuading each other and students to join the hostile mob was through unethical communication that included spreading gossip and rumors, undervaluation of the target faculty member's work efforts, and verbal harassment. Recruiting other faculty members and students to gang up in a mobbing against another faculty member requires deliberate, concerted efforts to spread negative information about the target.

This kind of unethical communication that is so commonly engaged in among members of groups in workplace mobbings is difficult to stop. But it is not impossible. Raising awareness and providing education about the process of workplace mobbing are among the most useful and effective strategies to stop it. Here is a list of six red flags suggestive of group-based unethical communication:

- You notice an increase in the amount and intensity of negative information being spread about a coworker or other organizational member. The information is increasingly negative, pejorative, devaluing, and focused more on the person than on their work.
- You notice that the target person is increasingly described in black-and-white dichotomous terms as being "problematic," "not good for the organization," "not able to perform their work," "has personal problems," "is a troublemaker," "needs to be gotten rid of," "is dragging everyone down," "is not liked by peers," "is not respected by management," "isn't a team player," and the newest one "is a bully." People are immensely complex and are not reducible to such catchphrases. Such descriptions are part of the process of objectification and the rendering of targets as "other," making it easier to eliminate them.
- You notice that the target person is absent from more and more meetings in which they, their style, and/or their work product are discussed.
- You are invited to specially called group meetings, either on- or offsite, to discuss a target person without that person being present or even aware of the meetings.

- You notice that many people are saying the same thing about a target.
- You notice that you are receiving and hearing information about a person in the workplace that you would typically not be hearing about or receiving information about.

Gregory Bateson, the famous communications theorist, said that a part does not have control over the whole of which it is a part.[16] In a group, that means that a single person does not have control over the entire group. Although a single person does not have control over a group, a single person can influence the group. If you are a member of a group that you want to influence or change, the easiest place to start is by changing your own behavior. In the flow of unethical communication that is central to group behavior in workplace mobbing, you can influence or change the group by: challenging the information that is spread about a target; asking questions about its source and the intent of distributing it; suggesting that the information cannot represent the whole story and that more information is needed, including information directly from the target; and, if you have the courage, asking whether it is honorable and decent to be participating in the distribution of this sort of information.

In workplace mobbings, the wildcard is the group. The group is unlikely to be an organized subunit of the organization. It is more likely to be an emergent group that has come together for the purpose of mobbing and eliminating a target and will disband after its work of ganging up and mobbing is done or, in the best of cases, after its work is interrupted or stopped. Individual members of a mobbing group can slow down or even halt the process of mobbing by calling into question the nature and intent of the information and unethical communication that is being distributed, as described above, and by refusing to continue to participate in the ganging up process. While it is possible for the organization and for individuals to make efforts to try and repair wrongs that have been committed in the process of ganging up and mobbing a target in the workplace, it is much less likely that an emergent group will be able to do that.

Nonetheless, there are two potentially reparative actions that former members of a group involved in the mobbing of a target can consider doing in the interests of repair but only with the caveat noted below. The first is to acknowledge and apologize for one's involvement. The second is to tell the target what is being said about him or her and what kinds of meetings and other actions have been taken to undermine her or his position in the workplace. One of the most disturbing aspects of the mobbing experience for its victims is to know that they are being excluded and undermined but also kept in the dark as to its full nature and extent.

Think what might have been different for the Turkish faculty member in the example above if one or two of the students or other faculty who were members of the group that ganged up had realized what was happening, discontinued their involvement in the group, and told the target what they knew about what was going on. Such information would permit the target to respond and try and protect his or her job or position but on a much more even playing field. It must be noted, however, that these potentially reparative actions at the group level are uncharted territory, and it is not possible to predict the outcome in specific cases. The principle of "do no harm" or, in the case of former members of a group involved in mobbing, "do no more harm" must prevail.

Individual(s)

Individuals have the greatest degree of freedom in altering course if they become involved in workplace mobbing. They can choose to stop participating in unethical communication and other aggressive acts against a target in the workplace. They can stop justifying and rationalizing their actions and can imagine what it would be like to be the target of workplace abuse and mobbing. They can make a personal ethical decision and stop participating. They can also commit to an ethic of transparent communication. A good way of operationalizing such transparent communication is to only talk about another in his or her absence in the same way that one would talk about the person in his or her presence. Following such an ethic of transparent communication would probably prevent most workplace mobbing from getting fueled in the first place. For individuals involved in workplace mobbing, reparative actions are the refusal to continue participating and the offering of a personal unqualified apology.

Restoring Victims to Wholeness

Workplace mobbing subjects victims to the threat of job loss and the cascade of personal and family insecurity and damage that goes with it. It also involves the psychosocial experiences of rejection, social exclusion, and ostracism—among the most difficult and challenging experiences for human beings whose very survival depends on affiliation with a group. Mobbing frequently results in damage to physical and psychological health and increases the risk that a victim will experience trauma as a devastating aftermath of being mobbed. There is widespread acknowledgment of the importance of efforts to restore victims of crime to wholeness. There is little to no acknowledgment of which we are aware of the parallel importance of restoring victims of workplace mobbing, whose losses are multiple and severe, to wholeness. We raise this topic not as an ending to our book but as an opening to a further conversation about workplace mobbing that we believe we all must have.

Restoring victims of workplace mobbing to wholeness requires a process of repair that is both symbolic and actual. We offer here a beginning template for what is involved, knowing that this conversation must be developed further and continued. The concept of restoration to wholeness is itself partially symbolic insofar as it is impossible to return a victim of workplace mobbing to life as it was before he or she was mobbed. Any workplace mobbing victim will tell you that there is no going back to life as it was before, no matter how much money a victim might have received in compensation (and currently very few victims receive compensation of any kind). But it is unethical to leave such victims out there unacknowledged and left dangling with their work and personal lives shattered.

So what are the elements of repair needed to try and restore a workplace mobbing victim to some kind of wholeness? We see the following four as a good starting point for reflection, conversation, and corrective action:

- Acknowledgment
- Apology
- Reparation
- Compensation

Acknowledgment requires naming that a wrong was done and that workplace mobbing occurred. This is important for mobbing victims who typically have been blamed for both the conflict and the negative outcome and who typically have also been told by HR and other management representatives that their grievances had been taken seriously when they were not. Suggestions are also frequently made to mobbing victims that they are imagining things and that there is no negative action being taken against them when the opposite is the case. Acknowledgment provides some measure of redress for such injuries of denial.

Mobbing represents abusive psychological and social behavior that can result in profound emotional harm. Apology is the offering of emotional reparation for an emotional harm. Such emotional reparation, although insufficient, is critical for emotional repair. Some form of emotional reparation is important for a mobbing victim, and material compensation cannot substitute for it adequately, if at all.

Reparation involves, at the least, efforts to repair the organizational and social fabric so that mobbing is prevented in the future. It is important for mobbing victims to know that their experiences at least triggered organizationally constructive actions to reduce and prevent mobbing from happening to others. Other forms of reparation to individual victims include providing them with information about details of what happened that had been kept from them so that they don't feel as if they are still in the dark. Such reparative measures serve the interest of helping mobbing victims reclaim their dignity and status. Other reparative actions might include offering a job back, offering a job in a different part of the organization (which is often preferable), and providing a meaningful letter of reference that would enable a mobbing victim to have a better chance at obtaining other needed work.

Compensation involves money and other material resources such as health insurance that were lost as a result of having been mobbed. While there is no returning to life as it was before mobbing, mobbing victims can be helped to return to some measure of wholeness through the kinds of restorative actions we have outlined here.

Emotional trauma is the most significant legacy of having been mobbed. We want to end both this chapter and this book with the astute observation of the late psychotherapist Michael White. He saw those who remained in distress as a result of their trauma as conscientious objectors to things as they are and who, in their pain, pointed the way to things as they could be. White said:

> Psychological pain and emotional distress might be understood to
> be elements of a legacy expressed by people who, in the face of the

nonresponsiveness of the world around them, remain resolute in their determination that the trauma that they and others have gone through will not be for nothing—that things must change on account of what they have gone through. According to this understanding, despite the absence of a wider acknowledgment that things must change, these people are sentinels who will not let this matter drop, and who have remained on guard against forces that would be diminishing of their experiences, and that would be reproducing of trauma in the lives of others.[17]

Appendix
Helpful Websites about Mobbing, Bullying, Trauma, and Related Topics

(Websites are filed alphabetically under each heading. All links were active at the time the book went to press.)

Workplace Mobbing

The Mobbing Encyclopedia (Website of Heinz Leymann)
http://www.leymann.se/

The Mobbing Portal
http://www.mobbingportal.com/

Mobbing.ca (Mobbing-Canada)
http://members.shaw.ca/mobbing/mobbingCA/index.htm

Mobbing-USA
http://www.mobbing-usa.com/Resources.html

Website of Janice Harper
http://www.janice-harper.com/

Workplace Mobbing in Academe (Website of Kenneth Westhues)
http://arts.uwaterloo.ca/~kwesthue/mobbing.htm

Workplace Mobbing Australia
http://www.workplacemobbing.com/mobbing.html

Workplace Bullying

Bullying of Academics in Higher Education
http://bulliedacademics.blogspot.com/

Bully OnLine (Website of Tim Field and the Tim Field Foundation)
http://www.bullyonline.org/

Project for Wellness and Work Life (PWWL) of Arizona State University
Hugh Downs School of Human Communication White Paper

"How to Bust the Office Bully: Eight Tactics for Explaining Workplace
Abuse to Decision-Makers," by Sarah J. Tracy, Jess K. Alberts, and
Kendra Dyanne Rivera
http://humancommunication.clas.asu.edu/files/HowtoBusttheOffice
Bully.pdf

Our Bully Pulpit on Workplace Bullying (Website of Beverly Peterson)
http://bullyinworkplace.com/tag/beverly-peterson/

The Workplace Bullying Institute (Website of Gary and
Ruth Namie)
http://www.workplacebullying.org/

Freedom of Speech, Suppression of Dissent, and Whistleblowing

Bullying, Harassment, Victimisation, and Discrimination in the
Australian Public Service (APS)

(Focus on the use of psychiatric referrals against workplace complainants and whistleblowers)
http://www.apsbullying.com/index.html

Foundation for Individual Rights in Education
http://thefire.org/people/3439.html

Government Accountability Project
http://www.whistleblower.org/

OZLOOP: The Australian Public Service (APS) Knows That Compulsory Psychiatric Referrals Are Unlawful, Unethical and Abusive
http://apsozloop.ning.com/profiles/blogs/the-aps-knows-that-compulsory-medical-referrals-are-unlawful

Suppression of Dissent (Website of Brian Martin)
http://www.bmartin.cc/dissent/

Business and Organizational Ethics

Bentley University Center for Business Ethics
http://www.bentley.edu/centers/center-for-business-ethics

Center for the Study of Ethics in the Professions
http://ethics.iit.edu/

Ethics and Compliance Officer Association
http://www.theecoa.org/imis15/ECOAPublic/

Ethics Resource Center
www.ethics.org

International Ombudsman Association
http://www.ombudsassociation.org/

Legal Issues in Workplace Mobbing/Bullying

Minding the Workplace (The New Workplace Institute Blog by David Yamada)
http://newworkplace.wordpress.com/

Workplace Health and Safety

Canadian Centre for Occupational Health and Safety
http://www.ccohs.ca/

International Labor Organization
http://www.ilo.org/global/lang—en/index.htm

U.S. Department of Labor Occupational Safety and Health Administration
http://www.osha.gov/

Parenting under Pressure

Australian Childhood Foundation
http://www.kidscount.com.au/english/chapter24.asp

When a Child's Parent Has PTSD: National Center for PTSD
U.S. Department of Veterans Affairs
http://www.ptsd.va.gov/public/pages/children-of-vets-adults-ptsd.asp

Trauma-Informed Health Care

The GlassBook Project
http://www.glassbookproject.org/

The Israel Center for the Treatment of Psychotrauma
http://www.traumaweb.org/

National Center for Trauma-Informed Care of the Substance Abuse
and Mental Health Services Administration (SAMHSA)
http://www.samhsa.gov/nctic/

Trauma Center at Justice Resource Institute
http://www.traumacenter.org/

The Sidran Institute: Traumatic Stress Education and Advocacy
http://www.sidran.org/

Somatic Experiencing Trauma Institute
http://www.traumahealing.com/

Trauma Soma (Website of Robert Scaer)
http://www.traumasoma.com/

Social Exclusion and Ostracism

Faculty Homepage of Geoff MacDonald
http://web.psych.utoronto.ca/gmacdonald/Publications.html

Faculty Homepage of Mark Leary
http://www.duke.edu/~leary/

Faculty Homepage of Naomi Eisenberger
http://www.psych.ucla.edu/faculty/faculty_page?id=98&area=7

Faculty Homepage of Roy Baumeister
http://www.psy.fsu.edu/faculty/baumeister.dp.html

Kellogg Insight: Downplaying Social Pain
http://insight.kellogg.northwestern.edu/index.php/Kellogg/article/
downplaying_social_pain/

Social Psychology Network: Kip Williams
http://williams.socialpsychology.org/

Wellness and Work Life

Families and Work Institute
http://www.familiesandwork.org/

Project for Wellness and Work Life (PWWL) of Arizona State
University Hugh Downs School of Human Communication
http://humancommunication.clas.asu.edu/about/wellness_and_
worklife

Notes

Preface

1. Jones, E. E. (1990). *Interpersonal perception.* New York: Macmillan.
2. Jones, E. E., & Harris, V. A. (1967). The attribution of attitudes. *Journal of Experimental Social Psychology, 3,* 1–24.
3. Jennings, A. (2004). *Models for developing trauma-informed behavioral health systems and trauma-specific services.* Washington, DC: National Association of State Mental Health Program Directors & National Technical Assistance Center for State Mental Health Planning.
4. Eisenberger, N. I., & Lieberman, M. D. (2005). Why it hurts to be left out: The neurocognitive overlap between physical and social pain. In K. D. Williams, J. P. Forgas, & W. van Hippel (Eds.), *The social outcast: Ostracism, social exclusion, rejection, and bullying* (pp. 109–127). New York: Cambridge University Press.
5. Nordgren, L. F., Banas, K., & MacDonald, G. (2011). Empathy gaps for social pain: Why people underestimate the pain of social suffering. *Journal of Personality and Social Psychology, 100*(1), 120–128.
6. Leymann, H. (2010). *Workplace mobbing as psychological terrorism: How groups eliminate unwanted members* (S. Baxter, Trans.). Lewiston, NY: Edwin Mellen Press.

Chapter 1

1. Westhues, K. (2006). Checklist of mobbing indicators. Workplace Mobbing in Academe. Available at: http://arts.uwaterloo.ca/~kwesthue/checklist.htm
2. Bultena, C. D., & Whatcott, R. B. (2008). Bushwhacked at work: A comparative analysis of mobbing and bullying at work. *Proceedings of the American Society of Business and Behavioral Sciences, 15*(1), 652–666.
3. The Workplace Bullying Institute/Zogby International (2007, September). *U.S. workplace bullying survey*. Retrieved from Workplace Bullying Institute website: http://www.workplace-bullying.org/multi/pdf/WBIsurvey2007.pdf
4. Yamada, D. C. (2012, April). *Responding to workplace bullying: The role of the ombudsman*. Keynote Address at the Annual Conference of the International Ombudsman Association, Houston, Texas.
5. Jacquemetton, A., Jacquemetton, M., & Weiner, M. (Writers), & Uppendahl, M. (Director). (2008). Six month leave [Television series episode]. In M. Weiner (Producer), *Mad Men*. New York: AMCTV.
6. Haynie, J. M., & Shepherd, D. (2011). Toward a theory of discontinuous career transition: Investigating career transitions necessitated by traumatic life events. *Journal of Applied Psychology, 96*(3), 501–524.
7. Duffy, M., & Sperry, L. (2012). *Mobbing: Causes, consequences, and solutions* (p. 52). New York: Oxford University Press.
8. Jones, E. E. (1990). *Interpersonal perception*. New York: Macmillan.
9. Jones, E. E., & Harris, V. A. (1967). The attribution of attitudes. *Journal of Experimental Social Psychology, 3*, 1–24.
10. Martin, B., & Saint Martin, F. P. (2012). Mobbing and suppression: Footprints of their relationships. *Social Medicine, 6*(4), 218–226. Available at: www.socialmedicine.info
11. Glazer, M. G., & Glazer, P. M. (1989). *The whistleblowers: Exposing corruption in government and industry*. New York: Basic Books.
12. Fox, S., & Stallworth, L. E. (2003). Racial/ethnic bullying: Exploring links between bullying and racism in the US workplace. *Journal of Vocational Behavior, 66*, 438–456.

13. Friedenberg, J. E. (2008, April 11). *The anatomy of an academic mobbing. The First Hector Hammerly Memorial Lecture on Academic Mobbing.* The University of Waterloo, Ontario, Canada. Retrieved from http://arts.uwaterloo.ca/~kwesthue/frieden-hh.htm

14. Lutgen-Sandvik, P., Tracy, S. J., & Alberts, J. K. (2007). Burned by bullying in the American workplace: Prevalence, perception, degree, and impact (p. 854). *Journal of Management Studies* 44(6), 837–862.

15. The Workplace Bullying Institute/Zogby International (2010). *U.S. workplace bullying survey.* Retrieved from Workplace Bullying Institute website: http://workplacebullying.org/multi/pdf/WBI_2010_Natl_Survey.pdf

16. Quine, L. (2003). Workplace bullying, psychological distress, and job satisfaction in junior doctors. *Cambridge Quarterly of Healthcare Ethics, 12*(10), 91–101.

17. Yildirim, A., & Yildirim, D. (2007). Mobbing in the workplace by peers and managers: Mobbing experienced by nurses working in healthcare facilities in Turkey and its effect on nurses. *Journal of Clinical Nursing, 16,* 1444–1453.

18. Chen, W-C., Hwu, H-G., Kung, S-M., Chiu, H-J., & Wang, J-D. (2008). Prevalence and determinants of workplace violence of health care workers in a psychiatric hospital in Taiwan. *Journal of Occupational Health, 50,* 288–293.

Chapter 2

1. Westhues, K. (2005). *The envy of excellence: Administrative mobbing of high-achieving professors.* Lewiston, NY: The Tribunal for Academic Justice/Edwin Mellen Press.

2. Leymann, H. (2010). *Workplace mobbing as psychological terrorism: How groups eliminate unwanted members* (S. Baxter, Trans.). Lewiston, NY: Edwin Mellen Press.

3. Twenge, J. M., Baumeister, R. F., DeWall, C. N., Ciarocco, N. J., & Bartels, J. M. (2007). Social exclusion decreases prosocial behavior. *Journal of Personality and Social Psychology, 92,* 56–66.

4. Twenge, J. M., Baumeister, R. F., Tice, D. M., & Stucke, T. S. (2001). If you can't join them, beat them: Effects of social exclusion on aggressive behaviors. *Journal of Personality and Social Psychology, 81*, 1058–1069.

5. Scaer, R. (2005). *The trauma spectrum: Hidden wounds and human resiliency.* New York: Norton.

6. Leymann, H., & Gustafsson, A. (1996). Mobbing at work and the development of post traumatic stress disorders. *European Journal of Work and Organizational Psychology, 5*, 251–275.

7. Pompili, M., Lester, D., Innamorati, M., De Pisa, E., Iliceto, P., Puccinno, M., Nastro, P. F., Tatarelli, R., & Girardi, P. (2008). Suicide risk and exposure to mobbing. *Work, 31*(2), 237–243.

8. The poem "why I was mobbed" is an original poem written for this volume. It was inspired by a poem by Barbara O'Mary cited here. O'Mary, B. (1973). "Why I am getting fired." In *This woman: Poetry of love and change.* New York: Times Change Press.

Chapter 3

1. Sperry, L. (2009). Mobbing and bullying: The influence of individual, work group, and organizational dynamics on abusive workplace behavior. *Consulting Psychology Journal: Practice and Research, 61*(3), 190–201.

2. Mantell, M. (1994). *Ticking bombs: Defusing violence in the workplace.* Burr Ridge, IL: Irwin.

3. Einarsen, S., Raknes, B. I., & Matthiesen, S. B. (1994). Bullying and harassment at work and their relationships to work environment quality: An exploratory study. *European Work and Organizational Psychologist, 4*, 381–401.

4. Matthiesen, S. B., & Einarsen, S. (2001). MMPI-2 configurations among victims of bullying at work. *European Journal of Work and Organizational Psychology, 10*, 467–484.

5. Namie, G. (2003). Workplace bullying: Escalated incivility. *Ivey Business Journal: Improving the Practice of Management,* November/December, 1–6 (reprint # 9B03TF09) 201.

6. Wrzesniewski, A., McCaukley, C., Rozin, P., & Schwartz, B. (1997). Jobs, careers, and callings: People's relations to their work. *Journal of Research in Personality, 31*, 21–33.

7. Vensel, S. R. (2012). *Mobbing, burnout, and religious coping styles among Protestant clergy: A structural equation model and its implications for counselors* (Unpublished doctoral dissertation). Florida Atlantic University, Boca Raton, Fl.

8. Sperry, L. (1996). *Corporate therapy and consulting.* New York: Brunner/Mazel.

9. Duffy, M., & Sperry, L. (2012). *Mobbing: Causes, consequences, and solutions.* New York: Oxford University Press.

10. Denenberg, R., & Braverman, M. (1999). *The violence prone workplace: A new approach to dealing with hostile, threatening and uncivil behavior.* Ithaca, NY: Cornell University Press.

11. Howard, A. (2007). *Workplace homicide: Extreme reactions to toxic work environments.* Presentation for the Seminar in the Sociology of Work, Department of Sociology, University of Waterloo, Canada. Available at: http://arts.uwaterloo.ca/~kwesthue/howarda0708.htm

12. Moll, J., & Rosen, M. (Producers), & Chiaberi, E. (Director). (2010). *Murder by proxy: How America went postal* [Motion picture]. United States: Key Element Productions.

13. National Center on Addiction and Substance Abuse. (2000). *Report of the United States Postal Service Commission on a safe and secure workplace.* New York: Author.

14. Toufexis, A. (2001, June 24). Workers who fight firing with fire. *Time.* Retrieved from http://www.time.com/time/magazine/article/0,9171,1101940425-164280,00.html

Chapter 4

1. Davenport, N. Z., Schwartz, R. D., & Elliott, G. P. (1999). *Mobbing: Emotional abuse in the American workplace.* Collins, IA: Civil Society Publishing.

2. Leymann, H. (1990). Mobbing and psychological terror at workplaces. *Violence and Victims, 5,* 119–126.

3. Meynell, H. (2008, November). *How to destroy a don.* The Second Hector Hammerly Memorial Lecture. University of Waterloo, Canada.

4. Waldrop, S. A. (n.d.). What to keep in a separate file. *Netplaces Human Resource Management.* Available at: http://www.

netplaces.com/human-resource-management/personnel-files/
what-to-keep-in-a-separate-file.htm

5. Heathfield, S. M. (n.d.). What employers should not keep in personnel records. *About.com Guide to Human Resources.* Available at: http://humanresources.about.com/od/legalissues/qt/personnel-records.htm

6. Johnson, L. S. (2008, May). "Personnel files" may be broader than you think. McLane, Graf, Raulerson, & Middleton Professional Association. Available at: http://www.mclane.com/resources/article-detail.aspx?id=551

7. Hillard, J. R. (2009). Workplace mobbing: Are they really out to get your patient? *Current Psychiatry, 8*(4), 45–51.

8. Eisenberger, N. I., & Lieberman, M. D. (2004). Why rejection hurts: A common neural alarm system for physical and social pain. *Trends in Cognitive Sciences, 8,* 294–300.

9. Duffy, M., & Sperry, L. (2012). *Mobbing: Causes, consequences, and solutions.* New York: Oxford University Press.

10. Lutgen-Sandvik, P., Tracy, S. J., & Alberts, J. K. (2007). Burned by bullying in the American workplace: Prevalence, perception, degree, and impact (p. 854). *Journal of Management Studies 44*(6), 837–862.

11. The Workplace Bullying Institute/Zogby International (2010). *U.S. workplace bullying survey.* Retrieved from Workplace Bullying Institute website: http://workplacebullying.org/multi/pdf/WBI_2010_Natl_Survey.pdf

Chapter 5

1. Martin, C. G., Cromer, L. D., DePrince, A. P., & Freyd, J. J. (2013). The role of cumulative trauma, betrayal, and appraisals in understanding trauma symptomatology. *Psychological Trauma: Theory, Research, Practice, and Policy. 52*(2), 110–118.

2. Bonanno, G. A. (2004). Loss, trauma, and human resilience: Have we underestimated the human capacity to thrive after extremely aversive events? *American Psychologist, 59*(1), 20–28.

3. Ozbay, F., Johnson, D. C., Dimoulas, E., Morgan III, C. A., Charney, D., & Southwick, S. (2007). Social support and resilience

to stress: From neurobiology to clinical practice. *Psychiatry* (Edgmont), 4(5), 35–40.

4. Duffy, M., & Sperry, L. (2012). *Mobbing: Causes, consequences, and solutions*. New York: Oxford University Press.

5. Bultena, C. D., & Whatcott, R. B. (2008). Bushwhacked at work: A comparative analysis of mobbing and bullying at work. *Proceedings of the American Society of Business and Behavioral Sciences*, 15(1), 652–666.

6. Cassitto, M. G., & Gilioli, R. (2003). Emerging aspects of occupational stress. *La Medicina del Lavoro [Workplace Medicine]*, 94(1), 108–113.

7. De Vogli, R., Ferrie, J. E., Chandola, T., Kivimäki, M., & Marmot, M. G. (2007). Unfairness and health: Evidence from the Whitehall II Study. *Journal of Epidemiology and Community Health*, 61(3), 513–518.

8. Leymann, H. (2010). *Workplace mobbing as psychological terrorism: How groups eliminate unwanted members* (S. Baxter, Trans.). Lewiston, NY: Edwin Mellen Press.

9. Niedhammer, I., David, S., Degioanni, S., & 143 Occupational Physicians. (2006). Association between workplace bullying and depressive symptoms in the French working population. *Journal of Psychosomatic Research*, 61(2), 251–259.

10. Nolfe, G., Petrella, C., Blasi, F., Zontini, G., & Nolfe, G. (2008). Psychopathological dimensions of harassment in the workplace (mobbing). *International Journal of Mental Health*, 36(4), 67–85.

11. Pompili, M., Lester, D., Innamorati, M., De Pisa, E., Iliceto, P., Puccinno, M., Nastro, P. F., Tatarelli, R., & Girardi, P. (2008). Suicide risk and exposure to mobbing. *Work*, 31(2), 237–243.

12. Punzi, S., Cassito, M. G., Castellini, G., Costa, G., & Gilioli, R. (2007). Mobbing and its effects on health: The experience of the "Clinica del Lavoro Luigi Devoto" in Milan. *La Medicina del Lavoro [Workplace Medicine]*, 98(4), 267–283.

13. Tracy, S. J., Lutgen-Sandvik, P., & Alberts, J. K. (2006). Nightmares, demons, and slaves: Exploring the painful metaphors of workplace bullying. *Management Communication Quarterly*, 20(2), 148–185.

14. Westhues, K. (2005). (Ed.). *Winning, losing, moving on: How professionals deal with workplace harassment and mobbing*. Lewiston, NY: Edwin Mellen Press.

15. Yildirim, A., & Yildirim, D. (2007). Mobbing in the workplace by peers and managers: Mobbing experienced by nurses working in healthcare facilities in Turkey and its effect on nurses. *Journal of Clinical Nursing, 16,* 1444–1453.

16. Davenport, N. Z., Schwartz, R. D., & Elliott, G. P. (1999). *Mobbing: Emotional abuse in the American workplace.* Collins, IA: Civil Society Publishing.

17. Field, T. (1996). *Bully in sight. How to predict, resist, challenge, and combat workplace bullying.* Didcot, UK: Success Unlimited.

18. Bureau of Labor Statistics, U.S. Department of Labor (n.d.). *Occupational safety and health definitions.* Retrieved from: http://www.bls.gov/iif/oshdef.htm

19. Van der Kolk, B. A., Roth, S., Pelcovitz, D., Sunday, S., & Spinazzola, J. (2005). Disorders of extreme stress: The empirical foundation of a complex adaptation to trauma. *Journal of Traumatic Stress, 18*(5), 389–399.

20. Leymann, H., & Gustafsson, A. (1996). Mobbing at work and the development of post traumatic stress disorders. *European Journal of Work and Organizational Psychology, 5,* 251–275.

21. Boals, A., & Schuettler, D. (2009). PTSD symptoms in response to traumatic and non-traumatic events: The role of respondent perception and A2 criterion. *Journal of Anxiety Disorders, 23,* 458–462.

22. Gold, S. D., Marx, B. P., Soler-Baillo, J. M., & Sloan, D. M. (2005). Is life stress more traumatic than traumatic stress? *Journal of Anxiety Disorders, 19,* 687–698.

23. Scaer, R. (2005). *The trauma spectrum: Hidden wounds and human resiliency.* New York: Norton.

24. Herman, J. L. (1992). Complex PTSD: A syndrome in survivors of prolonged and repeated trauma. *Journal of Traumatic Stress, 5*(3), 377–391.

25. Lapierre, L. M., Spector, P. E., & Leck, J. D. (2005). Sexual versus non-sexual workplace aggression and victims' overall job satisfaction. *Journal of Occupational Health Psychology, 10*(2), 155–169.

26. Field, T. (1996–2009). *Bully online.* Available at: http://www.bullyonline.org/

27. Dalgleish, T., Rolfe, J., Golden, A.-M., Dunn, B. D., and Barnard, P. J. (2008). Reduced autobiographical memory specificity and

posttraumatic stress: Exploring the contributions of impaired executive control and affect regulation. *Journal of Abnormal Psychology, 117*(1), 236–241.

28. Eisenberger, N. I., & Lieberman, M. D. (2004). Why rejection hurts: A common neural alarm system for physical and social pain. *Trends in Cognitive Sciences, 8*, 294–300.

29. Twenge, J. M., Catanese, K. R., & Baumeister, R. F. (2003). Social exclusion and the deconstructed state: Time perception, meaninglessness, lethargy, lack of emotion, and self-awareness. *Journal of Personality and Social Psychology, 85*, 409–423.

30. Hochschild, A. R. (1997). *The time bind: When work becomes home and home becomes work.* New York: Metropolitan Books.

31. Haynie, J. M., & Shepherd, D. (2011). Toward a theory of discontinuous career transition: Investigating career transitions necessitated by traumatic life events. *Journal of Applied Psychology, 96*(3), 501–524.

32. Pearson, C. M., Andersson, L. M., & Porath, C. L. (2000). Assessing and attacking workplace incivility. *Organizational Dynamics, 29*(2), 123–137.

33. López-Cabarcos, M. Á., & Vázquez-Rodríguez, P. (2006). Psychological harassment in the Spanish public university system. *Academy of Health Care Management Journal, 2*, 21–39.

Chapter 6

1. Westhues, K. (2004). *Workplace mobbing in academe: Reports from twenty universities.* Lewiston, NY: Edwin Mellen Press.

2. Duffy, M. (2010). Recovering intimacy with regard to health, work, and friendship issues. In J. Carlson & L. Sperry (Eds.), *Recovery intimacy in love relationships: A clinicians' guide* (pp. 249–269). New York: Routledge.

3. Gottman, J. M. (2011). *The science of trust: Emotional attunement for couples.* New York: Norton.

4. Gottman, J. M. (1999). *The marriage clinic: A scientifically based marital therapy.* New York: Norton.

5. Kazdin, A. E. (2009). *The Kazdin method for parenting the defiant child.* New York: Mariner Books.

6. Siegel, D. J., & Hartzell, M. (2003). *Parenting from the inside out*. New York: Jeremy P. Tarcher/Putnam.

7. Taffel, R. (2010). *Childhood unbound: The powerful new parenting approach that gives our 21st century kids the authority, love, and listening they need to thrive*. New York: Free Press.

8. Leymann, H. (1990). Mobbing and psychological terror at workplaces. *Violence and Victims, 5*, 119–126.

9. Leymann, H. (1996). The content and development of mobbing at work. In D. Zapf & H. Leymann (Eds.), *Mobbing and victimization at work* (pp. 165–184). Hove, UK: Psychology Press.

10. National Research Council and Institute of Medicine (2009). *Depression in parents, parenting, and children: Opportunities to improve identification, treatment, and prevention*. Washington, DC: Author.

11. Yamada, D. (2012, May 21). *Trickle-down abuse: Workplace bullying, depression, and kids*. Minding the Workplace: The New Workplace Institute Blog. Available at: http://newworkplace.wordpress.com/2012/05/21/trickle-down-abuse-workplace-bullying-depression-and-kids/

12. Adoric, V. C., & Kvartuc, T. (2007). Effects of mobbing on justice beliefs and adjustment. *European Psychologist, 12*(4), 261–271.

13. Vartia, M. (2003). *Workplace bullying: A study on the work environment, well-being and health* (No. 56). Finnish Institute of Occupational Health, People and Work Research Reports.

14. Tehrani, N. (2004). Bullying: A source of chronic post traumatic stress. *British Journal of Guidance and Counselling, 32*, 358–366.

15. Watzlawick, P., Bavelas, J., & Jackson, D. (1967). *Pragmatics of human communication: A study of interactional patterns, pathologies and paradoxes*. New York: Norton.

16. Steensma, H., Hubert, A., Furda, J., & Groot, F. D. (2004). Ripple effects of bullying in the workplace on bystanders and family members of the target of bullying. *International Journal of Psychology, 39*, 393.

17. Notelaers, G. (2010). *Workplace bullying: A risk control perspective*. Doctoral dissertation, University of Bergen, Norway. Available at: http://unimaas.academia.edu/GuyNotelaers/Papers/455492/Workplace_Bullying_a_risk_control_perspective

18. Namie, G., & Lutgen-Sandvik, P. (2010). Active and passive accomplices: The communal character of workplace bullying. *International Journal of Communication, 4,* 343–373.

19. Paull, M., Omari, M., & Standen, P. (2012). When is a bystander not a bystander? A typology of the roles of bystanders in workplace bullying. *Asia Pacific Journal of Human Resources, 50,* 351–366.

20. Lewis, S. E., & Orford, J. (2005). Women's experiences of workplace bullying: Changes in social relationships. *Journal of Community and Applied Social Psychology, 15,* 29–47.

21. Van Heugten, K. (2010). Bullying of social workers: Outcomes of a grounded study into impacts and interventions. *British Journal of Social Work, 40*(2), 638–655.

22. Rayner, C., Hoel, H., & Cooper, C. L. (2002). *Workplace bullying: What we know, who is to blame, and what can we do?* London: Taylor & Francis.

23. Lutgen-Sandvik, P., Tracy, S. J., & Alberts, J. K. (2007). Burned by bullying in the American workplace: Prevalence, perception, degree, and impact. *Journal of Management Studies, 44*(6), 837–862.

24. Janson, G. R., & Hazler, R. J. (2004). Trauma reactions of bystanders and victims to repetitive abuse experiences. *Violence and Victims, 19*(2), 239–255.

25. Haley, J., Stein, W., & Dingwell, H. *The truth about abuse* (2nd ed.). (R. N. Golden and F. L. Peterson, eds.). New York: Facts on File.

26. The Workplace Bullying Institute (n.d.). *How employers pay.* Retrieved from Workplace Bullying Institute website: http://bullyinginstitute.org/education/bbstudies/econ.html

27. Pinkerfield, H. (2006, November). Beat the bullies. *Human Resources, 84*(11), 77–79.

Chapter 7

1. Jennings, A. (2004). *Models for developing trauma-informed behavioral health systems and trauma-specific services.* Washington, DC: National Association of State Mental Health

Program Directors & National Technical Assistance Center for State Mental Health Planning.

2. Nordgren, L. F., Banas, K., & MacDonald, G. (2011). Empathy gaps for social pain: Why people underestimate the pain of social suffering. *Journal of Personality and Social Psychology, 100*(1), 120–128.

3. Williams, K. D. (2011, January/February). The pain of exclusion. *Scientific American Mind, 21*(6), 30–37.

4. Williams, K. D. (2009). Ostracism: Effects of being excluded and ignored. In M. Zanna (Ed.), *Advances in experimental social psychology* (pp. 275–314). New York: Academic Press.

5. Eisenberger, N. I., & Lieberman, M. D. (2005). Why it hurts to be left out: The neurocognitive overlap between physical and social pain. In K. D. Williams, J. P. Forgas, & W. van Hippel (Eds.), *The social outcast: Ostracism, social exclusion, rejection, and bullying* (pp. 109–127). New York: Cambridge University Press.

6. White, M. (2007). *Maps of narrative practice*. New York: W. W. Norton.

7. White, M. (2006). Working with people who are suffering the consequences of multiple trauma: A narrative perspective. In D. Denborough (Ed.), *Trauma: Narrative responses to traumatic experience* (pp. 25–85). Adelaide, Australia: Dulwich Centre Publications.

8. Leymann, H. (2010). *Workplace mobbing as psychological terrorism: How groups eliminate unwanted members* (S. Baxter, Trans.). Lewiston, NY: Edwin Mellen Press.

9. Finkelhor, D., Ormrod, R. K., & Turner, H. A. (2007). Polyvictimization and trauma in a national longitudinal cohort. *Development and Psychopathology, 19,* 149–166.

10. Scaer, R. (2005). *The trauma spectrum: Hidden wounds and human resiliency*. New York: Norton.

11. Herman, J. L. (1997). *Trauma and recovery*. New York: Basic Books.

12. Neimeyer, R. A. (2006). Re-storying loss: Fostering growth in the posttraumatic narrative. In L. Calhoun & R. Tedeschi (Eds.), *Handbook of posttraumatic growth: Research and practice* (pp. 68–80). Mahwah, NJ: Erlbaum.

13. Duffy, M., & Sperry, L. (2012). *Mobbing: Causes, consequences, and solutions*. New York: Oxford University Press. The information in the section of this chapter entitled "If You Are the

Target-Victim: Some Guidelines for What to Do in an Ongoing Mobbing" is based on Table 11.1, "Designing a Personalized Plan for Recovery from Mobbing," of the cited work.

14. Twenge, J. M., Baumeister, R. F., Tice, D. M., & Stucke, T. S. (2001). If you can't join them, beat them: Effects of social exclusion on aggressive behaviors. *Journal of Personality and Social Psychology, 81*, 1058–1069.

15. Westhues, K. (2005). *The envy of excellence: Administrative mobbing of high-achieving professors.* Lewiston, NY: Tribunal for Academic Justice/Edwin Mellen Press.

16. Westhues, K. (2005). *The pope versus the professor: Benedict XVI and the legitimation of mobbing.* Lewiston, NY: Tribunal for Academic Justice/Edwin Mellen Press.

17. Westhues, K. (2005). (Ed.). *Winning, losing, moving on: How professionals deal with workplace harassment and mobbing.* Lewiston, NY: Edwin Mellen Press.

18. Van der Kolk, B. A. (2006). Clinical implications of neuroscience research in PTSD. *Annals of the New York Academy of Sciences, 1071*, 277–293.

19. Van der Kolk, B. A. (1994). The body keeps the score: Memory and the emerging psychobiology of post traumatic stress. *Harvard Review of Psychiatry, 1*, 253–265.

20. Van der Kolk, B. A., & van der Hart, O. (1991). The intrusive past: The flexibility of memory and the engraving of trauma. *American Imago, 48*, 425–454.

21. Martin, C. G., Cromer, L. D., DePrince, A. P., & Freyd, J. J. (2011). The role of cumulative trauma, betrayal, and appraisals in understanding trauma symptomatology. *Psychological Trauma: Theory, Research, Practice, and Policy*, DOI: 10.1037/a0025686.

22. Harper, J. (2010). *Just us justice: The gentle genocide of workplace mobbing.* Available at: http://www.janice-harper.com/Documents/Harper%20Just%20Us%20Justice.pdf

23. Meynell, H. (2008, November). *How to destroy a don.* The Second Hector Hammerly Memorial Lecture. University of Waterloo, Canada.

24. Hillard, J. R. (2009). Workplace mobbing: Are they really out to get your patient? *Current Psychiatry, 8*(4), 45–51.

25. Blanch, A. (2003). *Developing trauma-informed behavioral health systems.* Alexandria, VA: National Association of State

Mental Health Program Directors, National Technical Assistance Center for State Mental Health Planning.

26. Janoff-Bulman, R. (2006). Schema-change perspectives on post-traumatic growth. In L. G. Calhoun & R. G. Tedeschi (Eds.), *Handbook of posttraumatic growth: Research and practice* (pp. 81–99). Mahwah, NJ: Lawrence Erlbaum Associates.

27. Tedeschi, R. G., & Calhoun, L. G. (2004). Posttraumatic growth: Conceptual foundations and empirical evidence. *Psychological Inquiry, 15,* 1–18.

28. Neimeyer, R. A. (2001). The language of loss: Grief therapy as a process of meaning reconstruction. In R. A. Neimeyer (Ed.), *Meaning reconstruction and the experience of loss* (pp. 261–292). Washington, DC: American Psychological Association.

29. Neimeyer, R. A. (2000). Narrative disruptions in the construction of self. In R. A. Neimeyer & J. Raskin (Eds.), *Constructions of disorder: Meaning making frameworks for psychotherapy* (pp. 207–242). Washington, DC: American Psychological Association.

30. Donaldson, R. E. (1992). Cybernetics and human knowing: One possible prolegomenon. *Cybernetics and Human Knowing, 1*(2/3), 5–6.

Chapter 8

1. Jennings, A. (2004). *Models for developing trauma-informed behavioral health systems and trauma-specific services.* Washington, DC: National Association of State Mental Health Program Directors & National Technical Assistance Center for State Mental Health Planning.

2. Blanch, A. (2003). *Developing trauma-informed behavioral health systems.* Alexandria, VA: National Association of State Mental Health Program Directors, National Technical Assistance Center for State Mental Health Planning.

3. Leymann, H. (1990). Mobbing and psychological terror at workplaces. *Violence and Victims, 5,* 119–126.

4. Leymann, H. (1996). The content and development of mobbing at work. In D. Zapf & H. Leymann (Eds.), *Mobbing and victimization at work* (pp. 165–184). Hove, UK: Psychology Press.

5. Leymann, H., & Gustafsson, A. (1996). Mobbing at work and the development of post traumatic stress disorders. *European Journal of Work and Organizational Psychology, 5*, 251–275.

6. Van der Kolk, B. A. (2006). Clinical implications of neuroscience research in PTSD. *Annals of the New York Academy of Sciences, 1071*, 277–293.

7. Williams, K. D. (2011, January/February). The pain of exclusion. *Scientific American Mind, 21*(6), 30–37.

8. Williams, K. D. (2009). Ostracism: Effects of being excluded and ignored. In M. Zanna (Ed.), *Advances in experimental social psychology* (pp. 275–314). New York: Academic Press.

9. Eisenberger, N. I., & Lieberman, M. D. (2005). Why it hurts to be left out: The neurocognitive overlap between physical and social pain. In K. D. Williams, J. P. Forgas, & W. van Hippel (Eds.), *The social outcast: Ostracism, social exclusion, rejection, and bullying* (pp. 109–127). New York: Cambridge University Press.

10. White, M. (2007). *Maps of narrative practice.* New York: W. W. Norton.

11. White, M. (2006). Working with people who are suffering the consequences of multiple trauma: A narrative perspective. In D. Denborough (Ed.), *Trauma: Narrative responses to traumatic experience* (pp. 25–85). Adelaide, Australia: Dulwich Centre Publications.

12. White, M. (September, 2005). *Workshop notes.* Adelaide, Australia: Dulwich Centre Publications. Available at: http://www.dulwichcentre.com.au/michael-white-workshop-notes.pdf

13. Schore, A. N. (1994). *Affect regulation and the origin of the self: The neurobiology of emotional development.* Hillsdale, NJ: Lawrence Erlbaum.

14. Herman, J. L. (1997). *Trauma and recovery.* New York: Basic Books.

15. Siegel, D. J. (2010). *Mindsight: The new science of personal transformation.* New York: Bantam.

16. Duffy, M., & Sperry, L. (2012). *Mobbing: Causes, consequences, and solutions.* New York: Oxford University Press.

17. Martin, C. G., Cromer, L. D., DePrince, A. P., & Freyd, J. J. (2013). The role of cumulative trauma, betrayal, and appraisals in understanding traumasymptomatology. *Psychological Trauma: Theory, Research, Practice, and Policy, 52*(2), 110–118.

18. Van der Kolk, B. A., Roth, S., Pelcovitz, D., Sunday, S., & Spinazzola, J. (2005). Disorders of extreme stress: The empirical foundation of a complex adaptation to trauma. *Journal of Traumatic Stress, 18*(5), 389–399.

19. Mollica, R. F. (2006). *Healing invisible wounds.* Nashville, TN: Vanderbilt University Press.

20. Yamada, D. (August, 2012). *Workplace bullying 2.0: When targets become change agents.* Minding the Workplace: The New Workplace Institute Blog. Available at: http://newworkplace.wordpress.com/2012/08/20/workplace-bullying-2-0-when-targets-become-change-agents/

Chapter 9

1. Sperry, Len (2002). *Effective leadership: Strategies for maximizing executive productivity and health.* New York: Brunner-Routledge.

2. Working at Google. (2012). *Glassdoor: An inside look at jobs and companies.* Retrieved from http://www.glassdoor.com/Overview/Working-at-Google-EI_IE9079.11,17.htm

3. Working at Starbucks. (2012). *Glassdoor: An inside look at jobs and companies.* Retrieved from http://www.glassdoor.com/Overview/Working-at-Starbucks-EI_IE2202.11,20.htm

4. Ferris, P. (2009). The role of the consulting psychologist in the prevention, detection, and correction of bullying and mobbing in the workplace. *Consulting Psychology Journal: Practice and Research, 61*(3), 169–189.

5. Catholic Health Services website. Retrieved from http://www.catholichealthservices.org/

6. Catholic Health Services: Patient satisfaction survey scores. Retrieved from http://www.catholichealthservices.org/about-us/catholic-health-services.aspx?nd=425

7. Stone, D. (Summer, 2012). St. John's helps set new national standards for nursing home care. *CHS Connections,* p. 1. Retrieved from: http://www.catholichealthservices.org/media/file/Connections/Summer.pdf

8. Ordway, D., & Hudak, S. (2012, September 10). Friend: Student submitted to hazing to gain respect. *Sun Sentinel,* p. 2A.

9. Allan, E., & Madden, M. (2008). *Hazing in view: College students at risk: Initial findings of the National Study of Student Hazing* (p. 2). Retrieved from www.hazingstudy.org

10. Ordway, D., & Hudak, S. (2012, September 11). FAMU faults drum major in his own death. *Sun Sentinel*, p. 2A.

11. FAMU's audacious explanation. (Editorial). (2012, September 18). *Sun Sentinel*, p. 10A.

Chapter 10

1. Heffernan, M. (2011). *Willful blindness: Why we ignore the obvious at our peril*. New York: Walker & Company.

2. American Psychiatric Association (2000). *Diagnostic and statistical manual of mental disorders* (4th ed., text revision). Washington, DC: Author.

3. Arendt, H. (1978). *The life of the mind: The groundbreaking investigation of how we think* (p. 180). Orlando, FL: Harcourt.

4. Arendt, H. (1963). *Eichmann in Jerusalem: A report on the banality of evil*. London: Faber & Faber.

5. Burton, J. (2010). *World Health Organization (WHO) healthy workplace framework and model: Background and supporting literature and practices* (p. 82). Available at the WHO website: http://www.who.int/occupational_health/healthy_workplace_framework.pdf

6. Shain M. (2009). *Stress at work: Mental injury and the law in Canada* (Final Report, Amended) (pp. 8–9). Paper submitted to the Mental Health Commission of Canada. Available at: http://www.mentalhealthcommission.ca/SiteCollectionDocuments/workplace/Stress%20at%20Work%20Mental%20Injury%20and%20the%20Law%20FINAL%20EN.pdf

7. Schore, A. N. (2003). *Affect dysregulation and disorders of the self*. New York: Norton.

8. Schore, A. N. (2003). *Affect regulation and the repair of the self*. New York: Norton.

9. Scaer, R. (2005). *The trauma spectrum: Hidden wounds and human resiliency*. New York: Norton.

10. Robbennolt, J. K. (2009). Apologies and medical error. *Clinical Orthopaedics and Related Research, 467*(2), 376–382.

11. Studdert, D. M., Mello, M. M., Gawande, A. A., Brennan, T. A., & Wang, Y. C. (2007). Disclosure of medical injury to patients: An improbable risk management strategy, *Health Affairs, 26,* 215–226.

12. Zimmerman, R. (2004, May 18). Doctors' new tool to fight lawsuits: Saying "I'm sorry." *Wall Street Journal,* p. A1.

13. Duhigg, C. (2012). *The power of habit: Why we do what we do in life and business* (p. 116). New York: Random House.

14. Ordway, D., & Hudak, S. (2012, September 11). FAMU faults drum major in his own death. *Sun Sentinel,* p. 2A.

15. Tigrel, E. Y., & Kokalan. O. (2009). Academic mobbing in Turkey. *International Journal of Behavioral, Cognitive, Educational and Psychological Sciences, 1*(2), 91–99.

16. Bateson, G. (2000). *Steps to an ecology of mind: Collected essays in anthropology, psychiatry, evolution, and epistemology.* Chicago: University of Chicago Press.

17. White, M. (2005). *Workshop notes: Attending to the consequences of trauma.* Adelaide, Australia: Dulwich Centre Publications. Available at: http://www.dulwichcentre.com.au/michael-white-workshop-notes.pdf

Index

The annotation of an italicized "*f*" or "*t*" indicates a reference to a figure or table on the specified page.

support needs, 140
talking it out, 102
fatigue and mobbing, 86–87
Ferris, Patricia, 168
Field, Tim, 80
fight, flight, or freeze responses, 24–25,
121–27
firing of target, 34, 122
Florida A&M University (FAMU),
174–76, 188
formal options against mobbing, 139
Fortune (magazine), 166, 167
Fortune 500 corporations, 165, 167
France, 16
fundamental attribution error, xv, 14–15, 37

ganging up in workplaces
conclusions, 36
conflict, out-of-control, 28–30
football coach case study, 20–23
getting rid of bully, 34–36
insiders *vs.* outsiders, 25–26
management failures and, 31–32
overview, 19–20
participation in, 183–84
process of, 33–34, 121, 190
warning signs of, 31
gastrointestinal problems, 78
gay, lesbian, bisexual, and transgender
(GLBT) issues, 97–99
gender differences in mobbing, 27–28
getting life back after mobbing, 153–58, 158*f*
Google company, 167
gossip
damage by, 66, 68
as unethical communication, 29, 31, 33
in workplace, 12, 20, 22
gossipmonger, 4
grapevine usage, 7, 12, 22, 117
grieving needs after mobbing, 119–20, 139
group dynamics
group pride, 41
in-group/out-group mentality, 8, 26–27, 50
insiders *vs.* outsiders, 25–26
of mobbing, xv–xvi, 37–38
pressure in mobbing, 183–84
repairing mistakes, 188–91

harassment
moral harassment, 16
nonharassment measures, 170
nonsexual harassment, 14
sexual harassment, 44, 169
Harper, Janice, 127–28
hate speech, 23
hazing rituals, 174–76

health benefits of employees, 71, 72, 120
health care providers, 130, 137
health concerns
of bystanders, 111
conclusions, 93–94
depression, 85–87
deterioration of, 72
effects on career path, 91–93
employee health, 164, 167–68, 177,
184, 188
gastrointestinal problems, 78
impact of, 1
increased arousal, signs and symptoms,
84–85
injuries from mobbing, 76–78
medical care needs, 129–32, 137
memory issues, 85
mental health impact, 1, 130, 185–86
overview, 75–76, 76*f*
physician's case study, 87–89
post-traumatic stress disorder, 77,
79–85
psychosocial impact, 89–91
sick leaves, 92, 112, 125, 136
sleep issues, 78, 84, 130, 158, 175
traumatic avoidance signs, 82–84
traumatic re-experiencing, 81–82
for trauma victims, 118
healthy workplace
accountability of organizations, 165–67
assessment of, 178–79
conclusions, 177
employee health concerns, 184
example of, 171–74
need for, 17–18
organizational health status, 164, 164*f*
organizational types, 167–71
overview, 163
psychosocial health of worker, 184–86
reflections on, 174
Healthy Workplace Bill, 12
"hear no evil" organizations, 169–70
Heffernan, Margaret, 181
Hochschild, Arlie Russell, 91
homicides, 1, 25
homophobia, 98, 100
Human Resources department, 68
human resources (HR) managers, 168
humiliation
degrees of, 117–18
from hazing, 175
by mobbing, 66–67, 92
parental concerns and, 104
recovery from, 133
types of, 122
in workplace, 20, 33